Shakuntala Recognized

Shakuntala Recognized

A Sanskrit Play by Kalidasa

Translated by G. N. Reddy

iUniverse.com, Inc.
San Jose New York Lincoln Shanghai

Shakuntala Recognized
A Sanskrit Play by Kalidasa

Published by iUniverse.com, Inc.

For information address:
iUniverse.com, Inc.
5220 S 16th, Ste. 200
Lincoln, NE 68512
www.iuniverse.com

This translation follows the manuscript in Sanskrit and Prakrit as edited
by V. P. Joshi in "The Complete Works of Kalidasa", E.J. Brill, Leiden, 1976.

ISBN: 0-595-13980-9

Printed in the United States of America

Contents

Introduction

Shakuntala Recognized was written in the Sanskrit and the Prakrit languages. Sanskrit belongs to the Indo-European family of languages. It may have originated in the central Asia, and in India, it matured and achieved technical sophistication by 1000 BCE. By 500 BCE it became an elite and courtly language. It produced diverse and brilliant works, which form the heart and soul of the Indian culture. Sir William Jones, the great British Orientalist of the late eighteenth century, described the Sanskrit language as "more perfect than the Greek, more copious than the Latin, and more exquisitely refined than either". This kind of refinement eventually led to its demise as a living language. Its variants, the Prakrit and the Pali languages became common.

One observes this demarcation in this play as well in the mode of communication between the nobility and the commoners. The noble characters use the Sanskrit language, while the commoner characters use the Prakrit.

This play was written, by the great poet Kalidasa, probably some time between the arrival of the Alexander the Great into India and 450 CE. Most scholars incline to put Kalidasa in the middle of the fourth and early fifth centuries CE. This time frame seems more plausible and it was also the time when Chandragupta II Vikramaditya and his successor Kumaragupta of Gupta dynasty reigned India.

Not much credible information is available about Kalidasa. He might have lived in Ujjain, the capital city of the kingdom. There are passages in his works, which suggest that he traveled extensively from the Northern Himalayas to the Southern dip of India.

Sir William Jones, a versatile man of broad knowledge, admirably described Kalidasa, in his preface to his own translation of Shakuntala Recognized, as "our illustrious poet, the Shakespeare of India". Ignoring the anachronistic appellation and ignoring the world of difference between the subject matters of these playwrights, one is struck by the genuine feeling of Mr. Jones in comparing thus. He took the great jewel of the English Literature, for that matter of the Western Literature, and bestowed that stature on Kalidasa. It is a bold attempt to present the great poet of a distant language and culture to an audience that was neither exposed to such literature nor willing to cede greatness to "alien" cultures. Seldom one risks oneself to rise above the provinciality of one's extant society. There alone lie the greatness and the courage of Mr. Jones, not in his recognition of Kalidasa as a great poet.

Mr. Jones' interest in Kalidasa could be attributed to an Indian pundit who introduced him to the play Shakuntala Recognized. The pundit quoted a few verses from the fourth act of the play to show that those were "eminently brilliant, [displaying] all the rich exuberance of Kalidasa's genius". Thus, Mr. Jones was inspired to pursue the play.

The following verses, from the fourth act, give us a glimpse of the romanticism of the human spirit, and perhaps explain why the play appealed to the German Romantics.

> *With the vanishing moon the memorable*
> *Beauty of lilies pales and fails to please my sight;*
> *Thus the sorrow of the endeared left alone*
> *By the beloved is unbearable beyond measure.*
>
> *On the eve of Shakuntala's departure,*
> *My heart is touched with sorrow.*
> *Tears bury my voice in the throat,*
> *Thoughts of her future blur my vision,*
> *Such a debilitating force in me,*

A hermit, all due to my affection for her!
What torment a father of the world endures
When he has to lose his daughter!

It is the deer, whom you healed with Ingudi oil,
When it cut its face with a sharp blade of grass,
And whom you fed with the wild mullet.
Like an adopted son, he does not want to let you go.

How can grief weaken me when I see the grains,
You scattered in offering, germinate at the cottage door!

Goethe admired the play when it appeared in a German translation, so much that he wrote the following poem, which appeared in the Deutsche Monatsschrift in 1791:

Will Ich die Blumen des frühen, die Früchte des späteren Jahres,
Will Ich was reizt und entzückt, will Ich was sättigt and nährt,
Will Ich den Himmel, die Erde mit einem Namen begreifen,
Nenn Ich Sakontala dich und so ist alles gesagt.

(If I want to depict the flowers of spring, the fruits of the later years, what appeals and delights, what satisfies and nourishes, the skies, the earth with one name, I will name you Shakuntala. Everything would have been said.)

Herder, who led the Romantics, wrote thus about the play:

Wo Sakontala lebt mit ihrem entschwundenen Knaben,
Wo Dushyanta sie neu, neu von den Göttern empfängt,
Sie mir gegrüsst, O heiliges Land, und du, Führer der Töne,
Stimme des herzens, erheb oft mich in Äther dahin.

(I greet you, O Holy Land, Where Shakuntala lived sequestered with her child, where Dushyanta regained her anew from the gods. You, the leader of sounds, the voice of heart, lift me to those celestial heights.)

Through their admiration, the play continued its European journey into many countries, inspiring many translations, musical scores, and operas.

Among Indian thinkers and writers, it elicited a new joy and pride. The European-style intellectuals of Calcutta compared the play to others in Western Literature. Bankimchandra Chatterji, who wrote the clarion song of the freedom fighters against the British, compared the character Shakuntala with Shakespeare's Miranda and Desdemona. A misguided attempt to confer the "greatness" of Shakespeare on Kalidasa! He missed the greatness of Kalidasa and thus the spirit in which Mr. Jones called Kalidasa as the Shakespeare of India. Shakespeare's Miranda and Desdemona do not grow like Shakuntala. Miranda's and Desdemona's are static relationships to the human condition; one pities them and moves on. Shakuntala's is a living relationship. Her femininity is not weakness but strength.

Rabindranath Tagore took one step farther in Indian pride and belittled the Shakespeare's play The Tempest with which he compared Shakuntala for the theme of spiritual journey. Again, such attempts betray the insecure and innate need to posit Shakuntala in the western literary cannon.

This need not be. This play is distinctly Indian, thriving on human qualities that the Ancient India prided in, such as sensuality, humor, passions and moral beauty. Indian sensuality far exceeds the Eros of the ancient Greeks. Only Kalidasa could suggestively evoke the beauty of the chest of woman thus:

> *Her tightly tied bark dress hides*
> *The beauty of her full bosom*
> *And the radiance of her youth,*
> *Like a sallow leaf, hovering a blossom.*

Or compare a woman to a blossoming vine thus:

> *Her lips the color of its sprouts, her arms delicate as its tendrils,*

Her youthful bloom fills her limbs, like a blossom a vine.

Only Kalidasa could see love in the languorous heaves of woman's behind thus:

When she steals a glance, even though at something else,
When her pumpkin hips languorously heave, as if with love,
When she pretends anger, as if her friend keeps her from leaving,
I imagine all to my cause. How love loves to see love!

The following verses describe Shakuntala as a unique individual. The poetic imagery and the psychology are breathtaking.

Born to a celestial nymph and a sage,
Abandoned by her mother, she was found
By chance like a fresh jasmine blossom
Carried by wind on to a dry grass plant.

Perhaps God painted her and breathed life into her,
Perhaps, he fashioned her from different mental forms.
When I look upon her exquisite beauty and creation
I feel as if she represents a new element of womanhood.

He notes that uniqueness and turns her into a sensual and sexual being delicately:

She is a fresh blossom intact on the tendril,
An unpolished gem and fresh nectar.
Her blemish-less beauty is the fruit of the good deeds.
I wonder whom Providence will allow to enjoy!

In an above verse he sees love in her ample behind, and he takes that image into an obsessive and fetish level in this verse:

These are her footprints,
On the white sand at the entrance;
They are shallow in the front
And deep at the heels from her heavy hips!

Even when he describes Shakuntala as tired and in love, he does not surrender her sexual physical attributes, a masculine perception he propagates willingly all through the play.

Her cheeks look emaciated, her breasts liquescent,
Thinned waist, drooped shoulders, pale skin,
Demeanor pitiful and fair, languorous with love,
Like a creeper stripped of its leaves by wind.

Leaving this bed of flowers,
Your breasts merely covered with a lotus leaf,
Why do you want to go into the sun,
When your limbs suffer with pain?

But then again, he is not an insensitive man and he is not afraid to express his sensitivity:

As I bury my head in my arms, night after night,
The tears that flow pale the glitter of the diamonds
Of this bracelet, which slips with ease the bow-scars
Of my wrist though I push it back over and again.

Shall I waft over you with this lotus-leaf fan,
A breeze moist with cool and refreshing spray?
Or, shall I take your lotus-stalk feet into my lap
And massage them until you feel happy?

Around the edges where my fingers pressed,
You see a streak of dirty smudge.
Here the paint swells to reveal
The spot where my tear fell!

The following poetic pick-up-line sentiment is not common place by any means:

Your untouched, soft lip, trembling like a new bud,
Seems, fair lady, to give me permission, as I thirst for it.

A person who could utter such lines could also show moral restraint when it deemed necessary.

I am offered a flawless beauty,
Not knowing whether she was once mine,
I feel like the bee trapped at dawn in jasmine:
It could neither enjoy nor leave the flower.

With the moon bloom the lilies of the night,
With the sun awaken the lotuses of the day.
Those who have control over their conduct
Would never embrace another man's wife.

In remorse at his act of refusal, he evokes an image of his beloved's state of mind and he burns in pain:

Rejected by me, she tries to follow her relatives,
But, the pupil of Kanva halts her.
Once again she turns to look at me with her tearful eyes.
Cruel me, it burns in me like a poisoned dart.

We do see his modesty even when his help was sought, and that was offered by him to a successful end.

In employing, for the success of a great task,
An agent, he reveals his esteem for the person.
Could dawn dispel the darkness of night,
If Sun, of thousand rays, had not engaged him?

The poet's imagination below is uncanny for a person from a pre-flight period.

The vagrant clouds dart through the spokes like birds,
The horses gleam in instances of flickering lightning,
The rims of the wheels are sprayed with moisture,
So we must be descending through the rain-pregnant clouds.

Landscape seems to glide off the mountain peaks,
Tree trunks thrust up denuding the cover of leaves,

Rivers, born emaciated, grow stronger and wider.
Do you see it? I feel as if the earth is being offered to me.

When the boy asks Shakuntala: "Who is he, Mother?" Shakuntala delivers the line: "Ask providence, my son." This is at once an expression of weakness and an expression of strength, for she understood the human condition. In that understanding she weeps instead of shouting at Dushyanta in anger. We must remember at this stage that she still does not know why Dushyanta rejected her. Dushyanta for his part falls at the feet of Shakuntala, an act of utter surrender with high cultural nuance. We must again remember that he does not know either why he forgot about his beloved.

Banish the sad thoughts of my rejection from your heart,
I acted cruelly under the spell of a delusion.
Under its dark influence I did not recognize the good fortune
Like a blind man, who rips a garland as if it were a snake!

Shakuntala in her infinite understanding says:
"Rise, my husband. I should have done something bad in my former life, which spent its force now. Otherwise, a compassionate person like you would not have acted that way."

She expiates her husband's refusal without even a hint of anger that one would expect at least at the moment of encounter with the person who caused her shame and agony. Calm and forgiveness should come later. But with her it is different. There she achieves a human perfection.

When she recognizes the ring, the *cause celebre*, he reciprocates by offering her it:

"Let the vine receive the blossom now to proclaim its union, as it is the season of spring."

There we have two unique individuals utterly suited to each other!

When the cause of all this agony is revealed he sees wisdom in her forgiveness. But then, it is a moot point. Her character had already achieved the sublime.

When one understands actions of people, one could even forgive a barbarian. But that understanding was not there in Prospero who seeks vengeance for his agony. That's what makes him an imperfect being, not capable of reaching the sublime.

In conclusion, Shakuntala Recognized is an Indian play and Kalidasa was a product of ancient Indian traditions, and the readers are encouraged to view it and read it in that prospective.

The Works of Kalidasa

Works of great artists are imitated by the less talented and there are always many of the less talented and ambitious artists. Consequently, many works were attributed to Kalidasa. The scrutiny of the works by critics over time, however, made the derivatives and imitations to fade in splendor; the real and the true stood out. Thus, only seven survived the scholastic rigor of critics as the genuine works of Kalidasa. Among those are three plays.

Malavikagnimitram: The King Agnimitra's father Pushpamitra, founded the Sunga dynasty, defeating the Mauryan king Brihadratha about 185 BCE. The saga of this dynasty lasted for more than a century. The play deals with a palace intrigue that unites Malavika and Agnimitra.

Vikramorvashiyam (Vikram[aU]rvashiyam) is based on the legend of how a mortal Pururavaas "conquered" the heavenly nymph Urvashi. The legend had its origin in a hymn of the Rigveda but was developed fully in Shatapathabraahmana.

Abhigyaana-Shaakuntalam (Shakuntala Recognized) achieved a unique harmony in weaving a fabric of human life with the threads of human frailties and tragedies. It was the first work to be translated into English and then a German translation entitled "Shakuntala" appeared in 1791. It was this translation that evoked the much-quoted admiration of Goethe.

The plot for this play is based on a tale in the Indian epic Mahaabhaarata. The tale depicts how India came to be called Bharatavarsha or Bharat, a name that is still official in the Indian languages. In essence the story is as follows: King Dushyanta, of Puru dynasty, while on a hunting expedition, meets the hermit-girl Shakuntala. They fall in love with each other. In the absence of her father, they marry by the ceremony of Ghandharva, a form of marriage by mutual consent with the nature (or its deification) as witness. They consummate their vows. When the time comes for Dushyanta to return to his palace, he promises to send an envoy to escort her to his palace. As a symbolic gesture he gives her a signet ring.

It so happens that when the irascible hermit Durvasa stops at her hut for hospitality, Shakuntala, in her marital bliss, does not hear his calls. The ill-tempered sage turns back unattended, giving her a curse that he who engrossed her in thoughts would not remember her. Time passes by and no one comes to take her to the palace. Her father sends her to the royal court for their reunion, as she was pregnant with Dushyanta's child.

Because of the curse and the circumstances in which she presents herself in the palace, Dushyanta fails to acknowledge her as his wife. Heart-broken, she pleads to gods to vanquish her from the face of earth. Her wish is granted. The spell is broken when a fisherman finds the signet ring in the entrails of a fish. The same ring that Shakuntala had lost on her way to the court. The king suffers from an intense feeling of guilt and injustice. Finally, he reunites with her. Shakuntala forgives Dushyanta and they are united happily. Their son is called Bharata, whose rule confers on India its name.

In the final act, Kalidasa distills the essence of human forgiveness through Shakuntala.

In addition to the plays, Kalidasa wrote two long epic poems: **Kumaara-sambhava** (The Birth of Kumaara) and **Raghu-vamsham** (Dynasty of Raghu).

The former depicts the events that lead to the union of Lord Shiva and Paarvatii, leading to the birth of Kumaara. The poem was never completed. Raghuvamsham is an epic narration of the ancestry and descendency of Rama, the hero of the Indian epic Raamayana. However, like Kumaara-sambhava, it was left unfinished.

Finally, there are two lyric poems: **Meghadutam** (or Meghasandesam) and **Ritusamhaaram**.

Meghadutam, which means the cloud messenger, is another perfect work of Kalidasa, both in the psychological and poetic mastery of the theme. It is a short poem of 111 stanzas. It deals with the psychological and emotional state of the mind of a Yaksha who was sent on exile for being inattentive to his duties. Thus separated from his wife he sends his message of loneliness, his longing for the union with her, and his concern for her state of mind. He sends this message with the cloud. The poem is an example of sophisticated mastery in describing delicately the innate primordial feelings. Besides, this work brings out well the lyrical fluidity of Sanskrit language. In this tone, Ritusamhaara, which deals with the birth and death of seasons, could be described as work of the maturing poet.

Characters

Dushyanta—the King;
His Charioteer;
Hermits;
Shakuntala;
Anasuya and Priyamvada—the friends of Shakuntala;
Kanva—the chief guru of the hermitage;
Gautami—the Mother Superior of the hermitage;
Sarangarava and Saradvata— the pupils of Kanva;
Durvasa—the infamous, short-tempered royal sage;
Bhadrasena—the King's general;
Madhavya—the court jester;
Vatayana—the chamberlain;
Somarata—the chaplain;
Vetravati—a female guard;
Chaturika—a maid servant;
Queen Hamsavati—one of the King's wives;
Police chief, and his two officers;
Fisherman;
Sanumati—a celestial nymph;
Matali—the charioteer of Indra, the chief of the gods;
Maarichi (also known as Kashyapa)—a holy sage, the son of Marichi;
Aditi—Maarichi's wife;
A Boy—Sarvadamana (or Bharata), the son of Dushyanta and Shakuntala;
And other minor characters such as hermits, servants, court poets, doorkeepers, servant girls, and a messenger.

Prologue
Benediction

He that sets creation with its first act,
He that is both the fire and priest of sacrifice,
He that is both the day and night, the two phases of time,
He whose element is the eternal sound of the cosmos,
He that is the source of all that grows,
He from whom every creature of nature draws its breath,
May he in his all eight forms
Protect you in his kindness!

(At the end of the benediction, enters the Stage Manager)

STAGE MANAGER:
> (*Looking off-stage*)
> Dear, when you are ready back stage, would you join me on the stage?

ACTRESS: (*Entering*)
> Here I am sir. Command me as to how I can be of assistance to you.

STAGE MANAGER:
> I see that we have a sophisticated audience here. Today, we present a new play by Kalidasa entitled Shakuntala Recognized. I hope everyone would play his or her role well.

ACTRESS: When we are so well instructed by you, there should not be any fear of ridicule.

STAGE MANAGER:

Dear, I tell you why.
Till the experts approve
My skills as a stage manager,
I cannot be sure.
Though one be well trained,
One cannot gauge one's own judgement.

ACTRESS: That is so true. Is their anything else you would like me to do?

STAGE MANAGER:

What else than to delight the audience with your singing!

ACTRESS: Of what season should I sing?

STAGE MANAGER:

None other than the relaxing summer season we are enjoying now. Because now:
Cool waters draw us to a delightful dip,
Forest breezes are redolent with the fragrance of flowers,
Every shade yields an easy slumber,
Day grows lovelier with every minute!

ACTRESS: Yes, in deed.
(*She sings*)
Acacia flowers, whose petals
Tremble as bees kiss the delicate stamens,
Are now picked with gentleness
By women to decorate their heads.

STAGE MANAGER:

Dear, it is a wonderful song! Now the audience is entranced like people in a painting. What can we perform to make it more enjoyable?

ACTRESS: Sir, you have already announced that we are pre-
senting a new play called Shakuntala Recognized.

STAGE MANAGER:

Oh, Dear! In deed I did. I completely forgot about
it for a second. Because:
I was totally drawn by the melody of your song,
As our king Dushyanta in this play by a swift deer.
(*They exist*)

Act I

(Enter King Dushyanta in his chariot armed with a bow and a quiver of arrows on his back, in the pursuit of a deer; his charioteer at the reins)

CHARIOTEER: *(Looking at the king and the chariot)*
The sight of you, armed and chasing after the beast,
Evokes an image of Lord Shiva himself on a hunt.

DUSHYANTA: This clever beast tires me like a mortal though. Look at him run!
With a majestic tilt of his neck, he looks at us with caution,
His hind parts tucked in lest our arrows strike him.
The cud from his tired mouth falls on his bouncing path
That lies vaguely between the sky and the earth.

(In surprise)
Now, where is he? I am losing him.

CHARIOTEER: We lost him on that uneven ground when I had to pull my reins for your comfort, my lord. However, he should not be far. We will gain on him.

DUSHYANTA: Then, loosen the reins.

CHARIOTEER: As you command, My Lord.
(He increases the speed.)
Look. My Lord!
With the reins loose, the horses race forth,

Ears upright, taut, plumes undisturbed,
Oblivious to the dust they gather up,
Galloping like tremulous winds.

DUSHYANTA: True! They indeed run with miraculous speed.
Distant blurry objects suddenly become clear,
Split images achieve cohesion behind us,
The crooked things shape into straight lines,
Nothing stays distant and nothing near.

I see him. Slow down!
(Dushyanta strings his arrow and aims at the antelope.)
(Voices are heard offstage)
VOICES:
The stag belongs to the hermitage. Don't kill! Don't
kill the stag!

CHARIOTEER: *(Looks and listens carefully)*
My Lord, Some hermits put themselves between
the deer and your arrow.

DUSHYANTA: Stop the horses!
CHARIOTEER: Yes, My Lord.
(He stops the chariot.)
(A hermit enters.)

HERMIT: *(Lifting his hand)*
O King! Do not kill the animals of the hermitage!
Do not ever discharge that arrow
Into the delicate body of the deer,
Like fire into a heap of flowers.
This deer is not a match for your arrows,
Which strike like lightning!

O King! Put back the arrow into your quiver.
It should defend the weak, not harm the innocent.

DUSHYANTA: I shall do as you ask.
               (He does so.)

HERMIT: This is indeed an act befitting a Puru.
               May you beget a son, a true scion of Puru,
               To be an Emperor of the heaven and the earth!

OTHER HERMITS:
               (Lifting their arms in benediction)
               May you beget an emperor for son!

DUSHYANTA: *(Bowing)*
               I am honored with the blessings of the hermits.

HERMIT: We came out to gather firewood, O King. You can see the ashram of our guru Kanva over there on the bank of the river Malini. If you do not have any other business, please visit us there and accept our hospitality.
               Witness our untrammeled holy rites,
               Protected by the security of your bow!

DUSHYANTA: Is your guru Kanva there?

HERMIT: For now, he put his daughter Shakuntala in charge of hospitality. He is away on a pilgrimage to Somatirtha to ward off an ill that awaits her.

DUSHYANTA: Then I will visit her. She will tell him of my visit.

HERMIT: Then, we leave.
               (They leave)

DUSHYANTA: Ready the horses, charioteer! I will cleanse myself by visiting the hermitage of Kanva.

CHARIOTEER: Yes, Your Majesty.
               (He starts the chariot.)

DUSHYANTA: *(Looking about)*

No need to be told. This is in deed the edge of an ashram for penance.

CHARIOTEER: How so?

DUSHYANTA: Do you not see? Look!

These grains under the trees
Fallen from the greedy beaks of parrots,
These oil marks on rocks
Formed from crushing the Ingudi nuts,
These trustful deer
That gaze undisturbed at our approach,
These puddles of water
Formed from the bark clothes hung to dry.

CHARIOTEER: Every thing fits.

DUSHYANTA: *(Having gone a little farther)*
Besides,

These water-channels ripple gently at the tree roots,
These sprouts are covered with the soot from the sacrificial fire,
The sharp shoots of Darbha grass have been cut in this grove,
These fawns graze indolently the delicate, soft grass.

We must not disturb the peace of the inhabitants. Stop the chariot here. I will get down.

CHARIOTEER: I will hold tightly the reins. Now, you can get down, Your Majesty.

DUSHYANTA: *(Gets off the chariot)*
One must be dressed appropriately for the hermitage.
(He hands the charioteer the ornaments, and the bow and the quiver.)

While I am at the hermitage, see that the horses are washed and taken care of.

CHARIOTEER: Yes, Your Majesty.

(He drives off.)

DUSHYANTA: *(Looking around)*

Here is the entrance. I will enter.

(He enters and pauses for a moment.)

In the tranquil steps of the hermitage,
My shoulder throbs,
What omen it portends!
But then, Fate has doors in all places.

VOICES: *(Offstage)*

Do not be silly! Come on this way, dear friends.

DUSHYANTA: *(Listens)*

I hear voices to the right of these trees.

(He goes forward and looks.)

These are the girls of the hermitage. They came to water the young trees, carrying pitchers that suit their own proportion. What a sweet sight!

Purity elusive to city-dwellers finds its right place here.
Even tended garden creepers pale before these sylvan vines!

I will observe them from this shade.

(He positions himself to watch.)

(Shakuntala enters with two friends, occupied as stated above.)

SHAKUNTALA: Come this way, my dear friends.

ANASUYA: I shall argue that your father loves these trees more than he loves you. Otherwise, he would not have asked you, who are as delicate as this jasmine flower, to water these vines.

SHAKUNTALA: I do not do this just for his sake. I have come to
                acquire a sibling's affection for the trees.
                (Looks at the tree with love.)

DUSHYANTA: So, this is the daughter of Kanva. He does not show
                good judgment in assigning her to the chores of the
                hermitage.
                In tasking such a lovely form
                To the fatiguing pious austerities,
                Perhaps the sage hopes to saw
                Hardwood with lotus petals!

                I will hide here behind the trees and silently watch
                them.
                (He does so.)

SHAKUNTALA: Anasuya, Priyamvada has tied this dress too tightly.
                Would you please loosen it?

ANASUYA: *(She does so.)*
                There!

PRIYAMVADA: *(With smiles)*
                Blame adolescence that swells your breasts. Do not
                blame me.

DUSHYANTA: Well said.
                Her tightly tied bark dress hides
                The beauty of her full bosom
                And the radiance of her youth,
                Like a sallow leaf, hovering a blossom.

                Yet, the bark dress, undesirable as it is, still has cer-
                tain ornamental charm.
                The mired weed enhances the beauty of lotus,
                The blemishes in the moon high-light its charm;
                Thus, the bark cloth makes her more enchanting.
                What does in deed not aid a graceful form!

SHAKUNTALA: *(Looking ahead)*
The shoots of that Kesava tree wafting in breeze seem to beckon me. I will go there.
(She does so.)

PRIYAMVADA: Shakuntala, stand still for a moment there.

SHAKUNTALA: What for?

PRIYAMVADA: You beside it like a vine, the Kesava tree gleams to have found its spouse.

SHAKUNTALA: Now, I know how you got your name—the flatterer.

DUSHYANTA: Priyamvada is not flattering her at all.
Her lips the color of its sprouts, her arms delicate as its tendrils,
Her youthful bloom fills her limbs, like a blossom a vine.

ANASUYA: Shakuntala, here is your true bride, twining this tree—the jasmine vine you call the "forest-flame".

SHAKUNTALA: *(Goes and looks at the vine)*
This tree and the creeper are well married. The young "forest-flame" is covered with fresh blossoms and the tree is growing strong with new branches.
(She contemplates)

PRIYAMVADA: Do you know Anasuya, why Shakuntala looks at the "forest-flame" like that?

ANASUYA: I cannot imagine. Tell me.

PRIYAMVADA: She thinks: "If only I could find a suitable husband, like the 'forest-flame'!"

SHAKUNTALA: You are just saying what you desire for yourself.
(She sprinkles water.)

DUSHYANTA: She must be the sage's daughter with a wife of another lineage. No doubt!
She must be suitable for the warrior class,
Otherwise, noble as I am, why would I desire her?

Nonetheless, in matters which involve uncertainty,
It is better to follow the inner inclination.

I must find out about her.

SHAKUNTALA: *(Agitated)*
Shoo this bee! This bee coming out of the jasmine flower is buzzing around my face.
(She acts disturbed.)

DUSHYANTA: *(Longingly)*
You touch her trembling eyes as they follow you,
You buzz softly as if to whisper secrets in her ear,
She waves you away, yet you drink her presence,
We seek, but you achieve the fruit of our search.

SHAKUNTALA: This thing does not go away!
(She moves away but the bee follows.)
It follows me wherever I go. Save me from this wretched bee!

BOTH: *(Smiling)*
We shall protect you? Call Dushyanta! This hermitage is under his royal protection.

DUSHYANTA: I will reveal myself now. Do not worry. Do not worry...
(He steps forward but then stops suddenly.)
I must not reveal myself yet. I must play a part.

SHAKUNTALA: *(Walks fast, glancing)*
It follows me everywhere!

DUSHYANTA: *(Emerging from behind the bushes)*
When Purus rule, controlling the unruly,
Who affronts the girls of the hermitage?

(DUSHYANTA's sudden appearance bewilders the girls.)

ANASUYA: Sir, it is nothing dangerous. A pestering bee disturbed our friend.
(She points to Shakuntala.)

DUSHYANTA: *(Looking at Shakuntala)*
Oh! Are the holy rites safe?
(Shakuntala remains speechless.)

ANASUYA: They are since we have a new guest. Shakuntala, go and bring this gentleman some fruits. I will wash his feet.

DUSHYANTA: Your gracious words are enough for the hospitality.

PRIYAMVADA: At least, you should rest for a moment under the shade of the Saptaparna tree.

DUSHYANTA: You must be tired from all that work. We will rest for a moment.

ANASUYA: We have to look after the guest, Shakuntala. Let's all sit down.
(They all do so.)

SHAKUNTALA: *(To herself)*
Why does my heart behave contrary to the values of the hermitage ever since I saw this man?

DUSHYANTA: *(Looking at them)*
I am glad to be surrounded by friends well matched in their youth and beauty.

PRIYAMVADA: *(Aside to Anasuya)*
Who is this majestic person? He speaks charmingly and with courtesy!

ANASUYA: *(Aside to Priyamvada)*
I am curious too. I will ask him.
(Aloud)
Sire, your gentle deportment encourages me to query you. Which lineage of royal sages do you

	belong? Which country repines at your absence? What brings such a refined being to our hermitage?
SHAKUNTALA:	*(To herself)* Stay calm. Anasuya asks him what I wish to know.
DUSHYANTA:	*(To himself)* Should I reveal myself? Should I hide myself? I will do the latter. *(Aloud)* I am an officer of the king touring these provinces with a duty to ascertain whether the holy rites at the ashram are proceeding undisturbed.
ANASUYA:	Holy men have a protector! *(Shakuntala displays sensuous shyness.)*
BOTH FRIENDS:	*(Looking at the demeanor of the other two)* Shakuntala, if only your father were here!
SHAKUNTALA:	*(With annoyance)* What is it then?
BOTH:	He will honor this guest's wishes, even if it is his life's delight!
SHAKUNTALA:	Stop you two. You have some silly notions. I will not listen to those effusions of youth.
DUSHYANTA:	Now I would like to ask something about your friend?
BOTH:	That would be an honor, sir.
DUSHYANTA:	The holy hermit Kanva is vowed to a lifelong-celibacy. How then your friend is his daughter?
ANASUYA:	I will tell you, sir. Have you heard of the great royal sage Kaushika?
DUSHYANTA:	Yes. We heard about him.
ANASUYA:	His daughter is Shakuntala. Kanva adopted her after she was abandoned.

DUSHYANTA: How so abandoned? I would like to know the cause.

ANASUYA: I will tell you, sir. On the shores of the river Gautami, Kaushika was engaged in stringent austerities that made the gods jealous. They sent the nymph Menaka to tempt and seduce him.

DUSHYANTA: Gods are in deed jealous of the deep meditation! What happened then?

ANASUYA: It was lovely spring time and seeing the intoxicating beauty of Menaka...

(She breaks off with shyness.)

DUSHYANTA: I understand the rest. The nymph engendered everything.

ANASUYA: Yes, sir.

DUSHYANTA: It's believable.

Neither could a mortal give birth to such a lovely form
Nor could a lightning issue forth from the earth's womb.

(Shakuntala droops down her head.)

DUSHYANTA: *(To himself)*
Now there is a chance to fulfil my heart's desire.

PRIYAMVADA: *(Looking with a smile at Shakuntala and then at Dushyanta)*
I am sorry, sir. Would you mind repeating it?
(Shakuntala waves her finger in reproach at Priyamvada.)

DUSHYANTA: Eager to know of good lives, I have another question.

PRIYAMVADA: Ask, Sir. We hermit dwellers are obliged to answer.

DUSHYANTA: I want to know about your friend.

Her ascetic life, a detriment to the thoughts of love,
Would it end with a marriage proposal?
Or would she end her life with ascetic vows
Among the deer whose eyes her eyes equal?

PRIYAMVADA: She is open to the suggestions of others, sir. But,
              her father is inclined to find her a suitable husband.
DUSHYANTA: *(To himself)*
              My prayers will be answered!
              My longing grows in certainty,
              What glowed like a fire afar is a gem by touch!

SHAKUNTALA: *(Angrily)*
              I am leaving now, Anasuya.
ANASUYA: Why?
SHAKUNTALA: I am going to tell Mother Gautami the non-sense
              Priyamvada is talking.
ANASUYA: But, it's not proper to desert a guest, Shakuntala.
              (Shakuntala goes away without heeding her.)
              (The king rises, but then checks himself.)
DUSHYANTA: *(To himself)*
              Acts do reveal the thoughts of a lover!
              Desire goes after her, but courtesy curtails.
              Unmoved, I seem to go forward and back.

PRIYAMVADA: *(Stopping Shakuntala)*
              It is not proper to go now.
SHAKUNTALA: *(Frowning)*
              Why is it not?
PRIYAMVADA: You owe me to water two trees. That is why? Pay
              your debt, then you can go.
DUSHYANTA: She is already tired from watering. Do not press
              her. Look!
              Her shoulders droop, her palms are red
              From the weight of the pitcher in her arms,
              Her bosom heaves strongly from the task
              That is too heavy for her delicate form,

The Sirisha flower decked behind her ear
Drenches itself in the sweat of her face,
Her tired hand holds the loose hair
That got liberated from the knot.

I will pay the debt for her.
(He gives a signet ring.)
(The two friends take the ring. They read the name on it, and stare at each other.)
Do not misunderstand me. It is a gift from the king.

PRIYAMVADA: In that case, do not deprive your finger of the ring. Your word is enough to clear her of the debt.
(Smiling)
This gentleman frees you. Or, is it the king? You are free to leave.

SHAKUNTALA: *(To herself)*
As if I want to go!
(Aloud)
Then, I will go when I feel like it.

DUSHYANTA: *(Watching Shakuntala, to himself)*
Does she feel for me the same way as I do for her? There is still hope for my prayers.
Though she does not respond to my words,
She lends her ears to my words.
Though she does not face me,
She does not look at anything at all.

VOICES: *(Offstage)*
Be attentive, hermits! Be ready to gather the animals of the hermitage. King Dushyanta comes on a hunt.
Dust stirred by his horses settles
On the bark clothes hung to dry

Like the red color of the setting sun.
It falls on the trees of the hermitage
Like a swarm of locusts.

And,
An elephant, unnerved by the King's chariot,
Carrying on its tusk a smashed tree trunk it lunged,
Dragging at its feet clusters of torn vines,
Enters our grove, scattering the deer of the hermitage,
And disturbing our austerities!

(All listen in fear)

DUSHYANTA: *(To himself)*
Good heavens! The soldiers apparently have disturbed the peace here. I must leave.

ANASUYA: This alarms us. Please allow us to go to our cottage.

DUSHYANTA: *(Anxiously)*
Please go. I will go and see if I can avert any damage to the hermitage.
(They rise.)

BOTH FRIENDS:
Sir, forgive this interruption to our hospitality. We are ashamed to ask you to visit the ashram again.

DUSHYANTA: Don't be. Seeing you has been of enough hospitality.

SHAKUNTALA: Wait, Anasuya. A sharp blade of grass pricked my foot. My dress is caught on a branch.
(Gazing at the king all the while, she leaves following her friends.)

DUSHYANTA: My interest to go back to the city diminishes. I will have my men camp here away from the hermitage. I just cannot remove the thoughts of Shakuntala from my mind.

Body propels forward, mind retreats
Like a silk banner drawn by the wind.

(All leave the stage)

CURTAIN

ACT II

(Enter the court jester with a forlorn look.)

COURT JESTER:

> *(With a sigh)*
>
> My God! I am fed up with being in the service of this hunting king. He goes off charging: "here is a deer, there is a boar, and over there is a tiger", endlessly in the heat of the high noon, in these summer days, down the forest tracks where not even a tree offers shade. When thirst overtakes us, we drink water from these tepid streams that smell foul with the dead leaves. We eat meals at odd hours with ill-cooked meat[1]. These horses and elephants make so much noise that I cannot sleep peacefully at nights. And then, even before the crack of the dawn these bastard huntsmen wake me up with the racket they make getting ready for the hunt. As if that were not enough, I have this pimple on my boil! Apparently, chasing after a deer, our king entered a hermitage and found this hermit girl called Shakuntala. Ever since, he has not said a word about going home. He

---

1. This passage alludes to the fact that Brahmins, the priest class, ate meat, in the ancient, pre-Vedic and Vedic times. By the time of the Upanishads the habit was abandoned.

seems preoccupied with the thoughts of her day and night. My providence! This worry had me tossing and turning in bed all night. I will go and see if he is up.

(*Walking about*)

Here comes our dear friend, surrounded by men carrying hands-full of arrows, young girls bearing garlands of wild flowers. I will stand here as if my organs are stiff with sickness. Perhaps that will get me the rest I need.

(*He leans on his stick.*)

(*The king enters as described above.*)

DUSHYANTA: (*To himself*)

My Love is yet hard to get; but her disposition eases me.
Love yet unrequited, when mutual, eases one's pain.

(*He smiles gently.*)

This is how a lover fools himself I suppose, imagining his beloved's thoughts to suit his own!

When she steals a glance, even though at something else,
When her pumpkin hips languorously heave, as if with love,
When she pretends anger, as if her friend keeps her from leaving,
I imagine all to my cause. How love loves to see love!

COURT JESTER:

(*Leaning on his stick*)

Your Majesty, my hand does not move so I greet you with words. Long live!

DUSHYANTA: (*Smiling*)

Why so paralyzed?

COURT JESTER:

> Why? You punch me in the eye and then ask me why tears?

DUSHYANTA: I do not understand.

COURT JESTER:

> Tell me sir, when a reed bends like a hunchback, is it by the influence of itself or the river current?

DUSHYANTA: Of course, it is due to the river current.

COURT JESTER:

> In my case, it is due to you.

DUSHYANTA: How so?

COURT JESTER:

> You give up all the stately matters, and hunt in this forest like a savage. I do not want to comment on that aspect. Since I am a Brahmin, these activities have paralyzed all the ligaments of my joints. That is how? I must take rest for at least one day.

DUSHYANTA: *(To himself)*

> That is what he wants. When I think of Shakuntala, even I am not enthused for hunting. Because...
>
> *I've no strength to string the bow to aim arrows at the deer,*
> *Which dwell near, and learn innocence from, my dear.*

COURT JESTER:

> *(Watching)*
> Your mind is lost in your heart's desires. And mine is lost to the forest.

DUSHYANTA: No, it is something else. I was thinking that I must listen to my friend's words.

COURT JESTER:

> Long live the king!
> (Jumps with joy)

DUSHYANTA: Stand still, and hear me through!

COURT JESTER:

> As you command, My Lord.

DUSHYANTA: When you have rested, I need your help in an untiring task.

COURT JESTER:

> If it's eating sweetmeats, I am ready now.

DUSHYANTA: I will tell you shortly. Is someone there?

> (The doorkeeper enters.)

DOORKEEPER: Yes, My Lord?

DUSHYANTA: Raivataka, would you ask my general to come in here?

DOORKEEPER: Yes, My Lord.

> (Exits and returns with the general)
>
> This way, sir. Our Lord stands over there with his commanding voice. Go near him, sir.

GENERAL: (Looking at the king, to himself)

> Hunting, though it is a vice, suits him like a virtue.
> *He looks thin, which masks his strength,*
> *Though his body is tasked hard in the hunt*
> *By the incessant stringing of the bow,*
> *By the sun, and the sweat.*
> *Like an elephant hidden by a mountain.*
>
> (Approaching)
> Victory to you, My Lord! The hunters have left for the forest. We await your word.

DUSHYANTA: General, Madhavya's disapproval of hunting kills my eagerness.

GENERAL: (Aside to Madhavya)

Keep to your word, while I try to change his mind.
(Aloud)
My Lord, he talks nonsense. We just have to look
at you.
Body grows nimble and fit for exertion, with fat free belly,
One observes animals distressed with fear and anger,
The mettle of an archer is proved with the moving targets.
With these qualities, it is wrong to call hunting a vice.

COURT JESTER:
(Angrily)
Go away, you instigator! My Lord is coming to his
senses now. Go and wander from one forest to
another until you drop into the jaws of a hungry boar!

DUSHYANTA: *(Addressing the general)*
Bhadrasena, we are near an ashram. I cannot
approve of what you said. For now:
Let the buffaloes in the cesspools churn the waters with
their horns,
Let the deer gather and chew in laze under tree-shades,
Let the resting boars dug out roots by shallow streams;
Also, let my worn-out bow stay unstrung for today.

GENERAL: As Your Majesty wishes!

DUSHYANTA: Call back the hunters, who have already left for the
forest. And ensure that the soldiers do not disturb
the sanctity of the ashram. Observe that
Through meditation, the hermits achieve solemnity,
Yet, they hide a potent energy that bursts into fire
At the provocation of another fire like the sun-stone
Pleasant to touch yet combusts at the stroke of the sun.

GENERAL: Surely, Your Majesty!

COURT JESTER:

There ends the story of the temptation.
(Exits the general.)

DUSHYANTA: *(Addressing his attendants)*

Go and change those hunting outfits. Raivataka,
You can go about your business.

ATTENDANTS: As you command, Our Lord.
(The officers depart.)

COURT JESTER:

You annihilated all the flies! Now you can sit down
on that flat stone under the shade of that tree. I
could also take the load off my feet.

DUSHYANTA: Lead the way, then.

COURT JESTER:

Certainly!
(Both walk about and sit down.)

DUSHYANTA: Madhavya, the true worth of having eyes escapes you
since you have not yet seen what is worth seeing.

COURT JESTER:

But, I see you right in front of me!

DUSHYANTA: Everyone sees oneself as handsome. But, I am talk-
ing about the cynosure of the hermitage, Shakuntala.

COURT JESTER:

(To himself)
OK! I shall not give him the chance.
(Aloud)
If the hermit girl is not obtainable what is the point
of seeing, anyway?

DUSHYANTA: Forbidden desires do not enter the minds of the
sons of Puru!

COURT JESTER:

Then, explain to me.

DUSHYANTA: *Born to a celestial nymph and a sage,*
Abandoned by her mother, she was found
By chance like a fresh jasmine blossom
Carried by wind on to a dry grass plant.

COURT JESTER: *(Smiling)*
As one sickened with the sweet dates seeks the sour tamarind fruit, you seek her because you are bored with the pleasures of the palace beauties.

DUSHYANTA: If you have seen her, you would not talk so!

COURT JESTER:
Something that engages your mind got to be special!

DUSHYANTA: What can I say about her, my friend!
Perhaps God painted her and breathed life into her,
Perhaps, he fashioned her from different mental forms.
When I look upon her exquisite beauty and creation
I feel as if she represents a new element of womanhood.

COURT JESTER:
She puts all other beautiful women into the shadow land!

DUSHYANTA: I think so.
She is a fresh blossom intact on the tendril,
An unpolished gem and fresh nectar.
Her blemish-less beauty is the fruit of the good deeds.
I wonder whom Providence will allow to enjoy!

COURT JESTER:
Make haste then before she falls into the hands of an ascetic with greasy hair.

DUSHYANTA: She is here, but her guardian is away, to seek his permission.

COURT JESTER:

        How does she behave towards you?

DUSHYANTA: By nature, these hermit girls are modest. However,

When I glanced at her, her eyes dropped.
When I engaged her otherwise, she smiled.
Restrained on account of her modesty,
She neither revealed nor hid her love.

COURT JESTER:

        Did you expect her to run into your embrace as
        soon she saw you?

DUSHYANTA: When she was leaving with her friends, she gave
        me an indication of her emotion towards me.

Pretending as if her foot was pricked by a blade of grass,
She stood still after having gone only a few steps.
Throwing her face around, she pretended to release
Her uncaught dress from the branches of trees!

COURT JESTER:

        She has given you something to think. You seem to
        have grown attached to this ashram.

DUSHYANTA: My friend, these hermits know me well now. I seek
        your advice to find an excuse to go the ashram.

COURT JESTER:

        What other excuse? You are the king!

DUSHYANTA: So?

COURT JESTER:

        Ask them for one-sixth of their grain as tax.

DUSHYANTA: You fool! The tax they pay from their meditation is
        more precious than the heaps of gems. Observe:

The wealth we get from the citizens is short-lived,
But the one-sixth from the austerities of ascetics is eternal.

VOICES: *(Offstage)*
                 We are here finally.

DUSHYANTA: *(Listens)*
                 These strong and calm voices must belong to asce-
                 tics.

GUARD: *(Enters and greets)*
                 Victory to Our Lord! Two young hermits wish to
                 seek your audience.

DUSHYANTA: Show them in.

GUARD: *(Goes out and re-enters with two young hermits.)*
                 This way please.
                 (Both hermits look at the king.)

FIRST HERMIT:

                 (To himself)
                 How radiant, yet how trustful he looks! This is
                 what is perhaps expected of a king who is almost a
                 sage himself.
                 Like hermits, he lives too, for the welfare of all,
                 He gathers merit by protecting his subjects,
                 By his virtue of control, he is lifted to the heavens
                 Like the sages, yet he is crowned also as a king.

SECOND HERMIT:

                 Gautama, is this the king Dushyanta, the friend
                 of Indra?

FIRST HERMIT:

                 He is.

SECOND HERMIT:

                 I thought so. I have heard a great deal about him.
                 No wonder he rules the earth to the dark limits of the
                 ocean,

*With his shoulders as strong as the keels of the gates of
a city.
That is why the gods seek for the success of their battles
His ready bow, and the thunderbolt of Indra.*

THE HERMITS:

(Approaching the king)
Be victorious, O King!

DUSHYANTA: *(Rising from his seat)*
Greetings to you both!

THE HERMITS:

Be healthy!
(They offer fruit.)

DUSHYANTA: *(Accepting)*
I am eager to hear you.

THE HERMITS:

We came to know of your presence, so we have a
request for you.

DUSHYANTA: What is your request?

THE HERMITS:

Since our guru Kanva is away, we wish not to be
disturbed by some evil spirits. Therefore we ask that
you come with your charioteer to take charge of the
ashram for a few nights.

DUSHYANTA: I accept readily.

COURT JESTER:

(Aside to King)
It is very convenient to get to your wishes.

DUSHYANTA: *(Smiles)*
Raivataka, ask my charioteer to bring my chariot
here, ready with the bow and arrows.

DOORKEEPER: Yes, Your Majesty.
(Exits)

THE HERMITS:

(With joy)
Your acceptance is in accord with the acts of your ancestors,
As Purus and holy kings indeed protect people in need.

DUSHYANTA: *(Bowing)*
You go ahead. I will follow your steps.

THE HERMITS:

Be victorious!
(They leave.)

DUSHYANTA: Do you now have enthusiasm to see Shakuntala?

COURT JESTER:

I was brimming with it until I heard the account of evil spirits; now it is all gone.

DUSHYANTA: Don't be afraid. I will be close to you.

COURT JESTER:

That would make me your knight-in-armor!
(A guard enters.)

GUARD: The chariot is here ready for your successful venture. The messenger Karabhaka from the queen mother has just arrived.

DUSHYANTA: *(In respect)*
Sent by my mother?

GUARD: Yes, My Lord.

DUSHYANTA: Show him in.

GUARD: Yes, My Lord.
(He exits and returns with Karabhaka.)
Here is Our Lord. You may approach him.

KARABHAKA: *(Approaching)*
Victory to you, My Lord! Queen mother reminds you that the ritual 'The fast of the Succession of

Son' is only four days away. She would like you to be at her side.

DUSHYANTA: Here is the request of the hermits; there is my mother's order. I must attend to both. What can I do now?

COURT JESTER:

Like Trishanku, stay put in the middle!

DUSHYANTA: I am seriously concerned.

Two deeds in different places split my mind
Like the current of a river divided by a rock.

(*Reflecting*)

My mother accepts you as her son. So, you go and explain to her that I am occupied with the protection of these hermits and that you would take the son's part in the ceremony.

COURT JESTER:

Do not think I am going away because I am afraid of the evil spirits.

DUSHYANTA: A high Brahmin like you, how could I think so?

COURT JESTER:

Then I shall travel as befits a brother of a king.

DUSHYANTA: Since I do not want the peace of this ashram to be disturbed, I am sending all of my troops with you.

COURT JESTER:

Then I will seem like a prince!

DUSHYANTA: (*To himself*)

He is a fool. He might let my inner desires out at the palace. So I must do something.

(*He holds the hands of the court jester and says aloud.*)

I am going to the ashram out of respect to our hermits. In truth I am not at all in love with the hermit girl. You see,

What do I have in common with her?
She was raised with the deer and is passionless.
So words I have spoken purportedly in jest
Should not be taken in a different sense.

COURT JESTER:

In deed!

(All leave)

CURTAIN

ACT III

Prelude

(A pupil of Sacrificial Rites enters.)

PUPIL: *(With joy)*
Dushyanta is in deed a great emperor! The moment he entered the ashram, all hindrances to our rituals ended.
The mere sound of the stringing an arrow on his bow distances
All obstacles as if it were the twang the bow releases.

I must carry this grass to the sacrificial fire.
(Goes forward, looks up.)
Priyamvada, to whom are you taking the ointment, fibers and lotus leaves?
(Listens closely and says)
What happened? Shakuntala is ill with the heat stroke and the ointment is to nurse her? Take care of her. She is the life-breath of our Master. I will also send holy water through Mother Gautami.
(He exits)
(The end of the prelude)

(Dushyanta enters, lovesick.)

DUSHYANTA: *(Looking worried, sighing)*

I am not new to the powers of discipline
And I know she is not independent,
Yet my heart dwells still upon her
Like water in a well, with no recourse.

(Showing pains of longing)
Cupid, you and the moon break the trust of the
lovesick!
They say your arrows are soft as flowers
And the moonbeams are mild and cool.
How contrary they seem in our experience!
For, the moon shines icy rays pregnant with fire,
And your flowers strike us like thunderbolt.

And so,
You cause endless agony, yet I invite you, O Cupid,
For, this smite of passion streams from my longing for her.

(He walks about.)
Now that all the troubles of hermits have been
taken care of, I must give my mind some rest.
(Sighing)
What else could give me the peace of mind than
seeing my dear? I will seek her now.
(Looking at the sun)
It is high noon. She would have gone to the
arbor-filled shores of Malini with her friends. I
shall go there.
(He goes forward, and with a shudder of joy looks)
How pleasant the flow of wind here!
Replete with the fragrance of lotus blossoms
And with the sprays of the ripples of Malini,
This breeze is conducive to embrace to ease

The languor, and discomfort of lovers.

(He looks around.)
Shakuntala must be in this arbor of creepers snug-
gled around by the bamboo trees. Because
These are her footprints,
On the white sand at the entrance;
They are shallow in the front
And deep at the heels from her heavy hips!

I will look through the branches.
(Goes forward and does so. With delight)
Finally my eyes attain Nirvana. There lies my
heart's desire, adorned with flowers, on top of a slab
of stone, attended by her friends. Let me listen to
their talk.
(He continues watching.)
*(Shakuntala and her friends appear as described
above.)*

FRIENDS: *(Fanning with affection)*
Shakuntala, does the breeze from the lotus leaf
comfort you?

SHAKUNTALA: What, are you fanning me, my dear friends?
(They look sadly at each other.)

DUSHYANTA: She appears to be very ill.
(Meditatively)
Could that be due to the heat? Or, am I right in
what I am thinking? *(He gazes at her longingly.)*
There could be no doubt.
Her anointed breasts and her lotus stalk bracelets
Make my dear's body, though ill, very beautiful.
Though heat and love cause the same discomfort,
Heat alone could not cause this in a youth.

PRIYAMVADA: *(Aside)*
                Anasuya, ever since Shakuntala saw the king, she is
                restless. There could be no other cause for her illness.
ANASUYA: That is exactly what my heart feels.
                (Aloud to Shakuntala)
                Dear friend, I must ask you something. Why are
                you ill?
SHAKUNTALA: *(Lifting her upper body.)*
                What do you want to ask?
ANASUYA: We do not know what goes on in your mind. You
                appear like the lovesick women we hear in the sto-
                ries. Tell us, why are you ill? To find cure one must
                know the cause of the sickness.
DUSHYANTA: Anasuya follows my logic. We see it alike.
SHAKUNTALA: *(To herself)*
                My illness is deep-rooted. How could I bare it all
                to you?
PRIYAMVADA: We mean well. Why hide what afflicts you? Your
                limbs emaciate every day. Nothing is left of you
                except your beautiful shadow.
DUSHYANTA: What Priyamvada says is true. She looks—
                Her cheeks look emaciated, her breasts liquescent,
                Thinned waist, drooped shoulders, pale skin,
                Demeanor pitiful and fair, languorous with love,
                Like a creeper stripped of its leaves by wind.

SHAKUNTALA:
                Whom else could I tell except you? I feel it might
                distress you.
BOTH FRIENDS:
                That is why we insist. Sorrow when shared among
                friends becomes bearable.

DUSHYANTA: *Implored by friends, who share her joys and sorrows,*
She could not desist to tell them the cause of her agony.
Though I have seen her often look at me with desire,
Now I can hear her say whether it was an illusion.

SHAKUNTALA: Ever since I saw the king, the protector of our ashram...
(She stops with embarrassment.)

BOTH FRIENDS:
Go on, dear.

SHAKUNTALA: Then began this plight—whenever my mind desires him, I become like this.

DUSHYANTA: *(With joy)*
I heard what should be heard.
Love, the cause of my torment, now brings me joy.
Like in the day, when the low-lying dark clouds,
Though add gloom to the discomfort of heat,
Relieve both by their inevitable showers.

SHAKUNTALA: If it meets your approval, I would like the king to have pity on me. Otherwise, you will have to sprinkle oil on my funeral pyre.

DUSHYANTA: Those words remove my doubt.

PRIYAMVADA: *(Aside)*
Anasuya, she has gone deep in this matter to lose any time. Besides he appears noble enough to be a Paurava. Could we do something about it?

ANASUYA: *(Aside)*
I suppose we could.
(Aloud)
Shakuntala, he is the right man to desire. It is natural for a river to flow into an ocean.

PRIYAMVADA: Like the Mukta creeper that needs the Sahakara tree for nurture.

DUSHYANTA: What is to wonder if spring follows the verdurous sprouts of branches!

ANASUYA: Priyamvada, what quick and quiet means could we use to fulfill our friend's desire?

PRIYAMVADA: About quiet means we need to think. But quick is as good as done.

ANASUYA: How so?

PRIYAMVADA: Remember, the king himself looked at her very affectionately with desire, and these days he looks emaciated with the lack of sleep.

DUSHYANTA: True in deed! That is how I look.
                As I bury my head in my arms, night after night,
                The tears that flow pale the glitter of the diamonds
                Of this bracelet, which slips with ease the bow-scars
                Of my wrist though I push it back over and again.

PRIYAMVADA: *(After reflecting)*
                We can write a love letter. I will hide it among flowers and have them delivered to his hands as offerings from the worship of Gods.

ANASUYA: I think it is a beautiful plan. What does Shakuntala think?

SHAKUNTALA: Whatever you plan I approve.

PRIYAMVADA: Then, think up a poem that will express your feelings.

SHAKUNTALA: I will. But my heart trembles with the fear of rejection.

DUSHYANTA: *(With smile)*
                I stand here eager for a union with you,
                You doubt me for the fear of rejection.
                We pray to the goddess to grant our wish,
                How could she not get what she desires?

BOTH FRIENDS:
> You underestimate yourself. Which idiot is going to hold an umbrella over him to ward off the glow of the autumnal moon?

SHAKUNTALA: *(With smile)*
> Then, I shall engage myself for the task.
> *(She sits up and thinks)*

DUSHYANTA: My eyes, without blinking, gaze transfixed at my dear.
> *One eyebrow engaged in thought, she composes lines*
> *While her face declares her love for me on her cheeks.*

SHAKUNTALA: I thought of a poem. But, I do not have anything to write with.

PRIYAMVADA: Here is a lotus leaf soft as parrot's breast. You engrave your love on it with nails.

SHAKUNTALA: *(Doing so)*
> Listen and tell me whether the message is clear or not.

BOTH FRIENDS:
> We are listening.

SHAKUNTALA: *(Reads)*
> *Your heart I do not know, but mine, day and night,*
> *Sets my limbs on fire in a cruel longing for you.*

DUSHYANTA: *(Approaching her suddenly)*
> *Love tortures your body but mine he burns to ashes*
> *Like the daylight that hides the moon but not the lily.*

BOTH FRIENDS:
> *(Arising with delight)*
> Welcome as our prayer's answer!
> *(Shakuntala tries to get up.)*

DUSHYANTA: Do not exert yourself!

The bed of flowers on which you lie is crushed,
The lotus fibers adorned as bracelets are bruised,
The feverish sickness that afflicts your body
Would not allow you to offer me hospitality.

ANASUYA: Would you please take a seat on this part of the slab here?

(The king sits down. Shakuntala remains shy.)

PRIYAMVADA: Your affection for each other is very apparent. Yet, as a dear friend to Shakuntala I must say something openly.

DUSHYANTA: Do not delay, my dear. Not revealing one's meaning may generate friction.

PRIYAMVADA: It is the duty of the king to protect the life of people in danger.

DUSHYANTA: None higher.

PRIYAMVADA: My friend has brought herself to this sad state because of her love for you. Therefore you should save her and nurture her back to life.

DUSHYANTA: My dear, ordinarily I am obliged to act so. In this case, I will give special attention.

SHAKUNTALA: *(Looking at Priyamvada)*

Dear friends, why do you bother our king with your pleas, when he must be pining for the palace ladies?

DUSHYANTA: O beautiful one!

This heart which seeks nothing other than to be near yours,
When you think thus, is wounded again by the love's
arrow.

ANASUYA: I hear that kings have many wives. So do not make my dear friend to be a grief to her family.

DUSHYANTA: What else can I say?

Though many wives surround me,

Two things will stand out in my clan:
The ocean-bound earth
And your friend Shakuntala!

BOTH FRIENDS:

We are satisfied.

PRIYAMVADA: *(Looking around)*

Anasuya, I see a lost deer looking here and there. He must be searching for his mother. Let us take him to her.

(Both leave)

SHAKUNTALA: Do not desert me! I will be alone.

BOTH FRIENDS:

Alone, when the protector of this earth near you?

(They exit.)

SHAKUNTALA: What? They left me?

DUSHYANTA: Do not be anxious. An admirer of you is near you!

Shall I waft over you with this lotus-leaf fan,
A breeze moist with the cool and refreshing spray?
Or, shall I take your lotus-stalk feet into my lap
And massage them until you feel happy?

SHAKUNTALA: I should not offend those whom I should respect.

(She rises up to go.)

DUSHYANTA: Beautiful lady, the day is not spent yet. Besides, you are weak.

Leaving this bed of flowers,
Your breasts merely covered with a lotus leaf,
Why do you want to go into the sun,
When your limbs suffer with pain?

(He holds her back with his arm.)

SHAKUNTALA: Please respect modesty! I am in love. But, what would others think of me?

DUSHYANTA: Do not be concerned about the elders. Knowing the rites, your father would not find fault with you. Because—

By the Gandharva rite, many daughters of royal sages
Have married their lovers whom fathers approved later.

SHAKUNTALA: Please release me from your grip. I must go and seek my friends.

DUSHYANTA: As you wish. I will release you.

SHAKUNTALA: Please.

DUSHYANTA: *Your untouched, soft lip, trembling like a new bud,*
Seems, fair lady, to give me permission, as I thirst for it.

(He lifts her face to kiss, but she turns her face away.)

VOICES: *(Offstage)*
The birds are coming home. The sun is setting.

SHAKUNTALA: *(Listens and is alarmed)*
Paurava, undoubtedly that is Mother Gautami coming here to know of my condition. You must hide in the branches.

DUSHYANTA: Yes.
(He hides himself)
(Gautami enters, with a pot in her hand, followed by Priyamvada and Anasuya.)

BOTH
FRIENDS: This way, Mother Gautami.

GAUTAMI: *(Looking at Shakuntala)*
Are you feeling better, daughter?

SHAKUNTALA: I am feeling better, mother.

GAUTAMI: Here is the water from the sacrifice. It will help you.
(She sprinkles water on Shakuntala's head.)

The day is departing. We must go to our huts.
(She leaves.)

SHAKUNTALA: *(To herself)*

Heart, when your desire was in your grasp, you hesitated. Now, you must bear the consequent pain.
(Taking a step and turning, aloud)
O creepers, you, who helped me to relieve my fever,
I leave now until better times[2].
(Shakuntala departs sadly with her friends.)

DUSHYANTA: *(The king emerges from his hiding place. Sighing.)*

Alas, what obstacles to overcome to achieve the goal!
The fingers that covered her lips,
The faltering words of negation,
The face turned aside in demur,
Yet I held her face, but alas no kiss.

Now, where shall I go? I stay a moment in this bower that sheltered my sweetheart.
(Looking all around)
The bed of flowers crushed by her body lies on this stone,
Here is the love message engraved on the lotus leaf by nail,
Here are the lotus-fiber bracelets that slipped her arm,
All these compel me to stay though this place is empty.

VOICES: *(Offstage)*

Where is the King?
As the evening libations are underway,
The sacrificial fire is densely covered
By fearsome, multitude of goblins,
Which look like dark clouds at twilight.

---

2. She bids the king good bye very subtly.

DUSHYANTA: I am coming there.

(Exits)

CURTAIN

Act IV

Interlude

(Anasuya and Priyamvada are seen on the stage picking flowers.)

ANASUYA: Priyamvada, though Shakuntala had married, by the rites of Gandharva, a suitable man of her heart's desire, my heart is not in its right place.

PRIYAMVADA: Why so?

ANASUYA: The sacrifices being over, the king is taking leave of the sages to go back to the city. I am concerned whether or not he would remember Shakuntala once he is among those palace ladies.

PRIYAMVADA: Be assured. People who are distinguished in character would not go against their grain. What must be of concern is how Father Kanva would react if he hears this account.

ANASUYA: As I see it, he would approve.

PRIYAMVADA: Why?

ANASUYA: His primary intention was to find her a suitable husband. That Providence provided with the least effort.

PRIYAMVADA: *(Looking at her flower basket)*
I think, we picked enough flowers for today's worship.

ANASUYA: A few more to wish for the welfare of Shakuntala.

PRIYAMVADA: In deed!
              (*They continue to pick flowers.*)
              VOICE: (*Offstage*)
              Hello! Does any one hear me?
ANASUYA: (*Listening*)
              Dear, a guest is announcing himself.
PRIYAMVADA: Shakuntala is in the cottage.
ANASUYA: But her mind is not in her. We must make do with
              these flowers.
              (*They exit.*)
VOICE: (*Offstage again*)
              This is an insult.
              Whoever's thoughts preoccupy your mind
              In neglect to my being here, though I am a sage,
              He shall not remember you even when reminded,
              Like a drunkard who cannot remember his words.

PRIYAMVADA: Oh no! Oh no! The unpleasant has happened. The
              blank-headed Shakuntala has offended someone
              worthy of respect.
ANASUYA: (*Looking*)
              Not just someone, who is worthy of respect! That
              was the short-tempered powerful sage, Durvasa.
              Having given the curse, he is walking away quickly.
PRIYAMVADA: Nothing else burns like fire. Go and throw yourself
              on his feet and beg him to return. Meanwhile, I will
              get some water to wash his feet in welcome.
ANASUYA: I will.
              (*She exits.*)
PRIYAMVADA: (*Takes a step and stumbles.*)
              Oh no! Walking hastily, I stumbled and let go the
              flower basket from my hands.
              (*She stoops to pick the flowers.*)

ANASUYA: *(Re-enters)*
                 Dear, he acted as if he is an incarnate of anger. Yet,
                 I mellowed him a bit.
PRIYAMVADA: That is indeed a lot. Tell me.
ANASUYA: Though I pleaded, he refused to return. I said:
                 "Your Holiness, since this is the first time it ever
                 happened, you should forgive this one ignorant
                 mistake of your daughter."
PRIYAMVADA: And?
ANASUYA: He said: "I cannot take back what I said. But when
                 he recognizes an ornament given to her by him, the
                 curse would be discharged." As he was saying this,
                 he just disappeared.
PRIYAMVADA: We can breathe freely now. There is that signet ring
                 with his name engraved on it, which the king him-
                 self put on her finger to remember him by. She has
                 her own solution.
ANASUYA: Then, let us carry out now our godly duties.
                 (They walk about.)
PRIYAMVADA: *(Looking)*
                 Look, Anasuya. Her left hand holding her face, our
                 dear friend looks like a painting. So engrossed in
                 thoughts of her husband, she does not pay attention
                 to herself, let alone visitors.
ANASUYA: Priyamvada, this incident should stay just between
                 us. We must protect our delicate friend.
PRIYAMVADA: Of course! Who will sprinkle hot water on jasmine
                 flower?

                 (They both leave.)

(The end of the interlude)

	(A pupil of the ashram enters, looking sleepy.)

PUPIL:

(A pupil of the ashram enters, looking sleepy.)

The reverend Kanva wakes me up at this hour to find out the time! I will go outside to see how much of the night is left.

(Looking about)

Well, it is almost dawn.

One side, the moon nears the western peak,
On the other side the dawn heralds the sun.
One splendor dies as the other grows.
How apparent the order of the universe!

With the vanishing moon the memorable
Beauty of lilies pales and fails to please my sight;
Thus, the sorrow of the endeared left alone
By the beloved is unbearable beyond measure.

(Enter Anasuya on the farther end of the stage)

ANASUYA:

Even people ignorant of worldly affairs would say that the king had not behaved like a gentleman towards Shakuntala.

PUPIL:

I will tell the master that it is time for the sacrificial fire.

(He leaves.)

ANASUYA:

Though I am awake, what can I do? My hands refuse to engage in the real tasks of the day. I hope the Cupid is appeased for letting the pure-hearted dear to meet such an unfaithful man. Yet, it must be due to the curse of Durvasa. Otherwise, why would the king, who said all those sweet words, not even send a letter until now? In that case, we should send him the ring he gave her as memento. But whom shall I ask among the worried hermits? We will get her into trouble if we go and tell Father Kanva that

Shakuntala had married Dushyanta and is pregnant. I have no clue to do anything.

(Enters Priyamvada)

PRIYAMVADA: *(With joy)*

Hurry, Anasuya! Hurry! We are arranging for the departure of Shakuntala.

ANASUYA: Dear, what?

PRIYAMVADA: Listen, I went to see whether Shakuntala had slept well.

ANASUYA: And?

PRIYAMVADA: I saw Father Kanva there holding our embarrassed friend. He was telling her: "The fruit of prayers has fallen into the hands of the worshiper though smoke covered his sight. I consider you like knowledge passed onto a good student. I will send you to your husband this same day with an escort of hermits."

ANASUYA: Priyamvada! Who told Father Kanva about this incident?

PRIYAMVADA: When he entered the ashram, a heavenly voice spoke to him in verse.

ANASUYA: *(Amazed)*

What then?

PRIYAMVADA: *(Quoting in Sanskrit)*

The seed of Dushyanta, for the welfare of the world,
Your daughter bears like the Sami tree carries the fire.

ANASUYA: *(Embracing Priyamvada)*

I am so happy for her. At the same time I feel sorry that Shakuntala would be leaving us.

PRIYAMVADA: Let us hide our sorrow. She should not become unhappy.

ANASUYA: Over there in that coconut shell hanging by the branch of the mango tree is a garland made from the long-lasting Vakula flowers, which I have been keeping for this occasion. You wrap it up. Meanwhile, I will make her some good-luck paste with the holy earth and the Darbha grass.

PRIYAMVADA: I will do it.

(Anasuya leaves and Priyamvada wraps up the flowers.)

VOICE: *(Offstage)*

Mother Gautami, tell Sarangarava to arrange a group to escort Shakuntala

PRIYAMVADA: *(Listening)*

Hurry Anasuya. The hermits are being ordered to go to Hastinapur.

ANASUYA: *(Enters with the good luck paste in her hands)*

Let us go, dear.

(They exit)

PRIYAMVADA: *(Looking)*

There stands Shakuntala, bathed at the sunrise, and being showered with the blessings of rice by the hermit women. Let us go near her.

(They go near her.)

(Enters Shakuntala as described above.)

FIRST HERMIT WOMAN: *(Addressing Shakuntala)*

May you obtain your husband's affection and become the queen!

SECOND HERMIT WOMAN: May you beget a warrior son, dear!

THIRD HERMIT WOMAN: May your husband love you deeply!

(They exit leaving Mother Gautami.)

BOTH FRIENDS:

(Approaching)

May you bathe in happiness!

SHAKUNTALA: Welcome, dear friends. Sit with me.

BOTH FRIENDS:

(Sitting down with the plate of good-luck paste)

Be still while I apply this good-luck paste on you.

SHAKUNTALA: So I become a bride again. I will never have friends like you.

(She drops tears.)

BOTH FRIENDS:

It is not auspicious to cry at good occasions.

(They wipe the tears off the face of Shakuntala.)

PRIYAMVADA: Your beauty deserves ornaments not this paste of hermits.

(Enter hermit boys with ornaments.)

HERMIT BOYS:

Here are some ornaments. Please, let Shakuntala wear them.

(Everyone is surprised)

GAUTAMI: Narada, where do these come from?

FIRST HERMIT
BOY: From Father Kanva's power.

GAUTAMI: From his mental powers?

SECOND HERMIT
BOY: Not quite. Listen. He asked us to pick flowers for Shakuntala. When we went:

One tree gave moon-white wedding dress,
Another oozed red dye to color her feet,
From others came, like the hands of fairies,
The graceful shoots full of ornaments.

PRIYAMVADA: *(Looking at Shakuntala)*
It seems like a good omen that you would be pros-
perous at your husband's place.
(Shakuntala shies.)

FIRST HERMIT
BOY: We shall leave, Mother Gautami, and tell Father
Kanva bathing in Malini about the gifts of the trees.

SECOND HERMIT
BOY: Yes, in deed.
(They exit)

ANASUYA: We have no experience in the proper use of these
ornaments. We have to do with what we have seen
in paintings.

SHAKUNTALA: I know your talent.
(They decorate Shakuntala with the jewels.)
(Kanva enters, having bathed.)

KANVA: *On the eve of Shakuntala's departure,*
My heart is touched with sorrow.
Tears bury my voice in the throat,
Thoughts of her future blur my vision.
Such debilitating force in me,
A hermit, all due to my affection for her!
What torment a father of the world endures
When he has to lose his daughter!

BOTH
FRIENDS: We are finished with you, Shakuntala. Put on these
cotton garments.
(Shakuntala does so.)

GAUTAMI: Daughter, your guardian, with eyes filled with the
tears of joy, awaits you. Go and get his blessing.

SHAKUNTALA: *(Shyly)*

	Father, my homage to you.
KANVA:	Dear,

May your husband hold you in affection
Like Yayati did his spouse Sarmishta!
Alike, may you beget a son like Puru
To form a dynasty to rule the earth!

GAUTAMI:	Sir, this is, in deed, a blessing, and not just a prayer.
KANVA:	Daughter, go round this sacrificial fire clockwise.
	(They circumambulate the fire.)
KANVA:	*(Reciting verses from Rigveda)*

May these fires of sacrifice sanctify you!
May the fragrance of fire from the altar
Decked with firewood and long grass
Repel evil and absolve you of your sins!

That will do.
(Looking on)
Where are Sarangarava and the others?

DISCIPLES:	*(Entering)*
	We are here, Master.
KANVA:	Sarangarava, you lead the way for your sister.
SARANGARAVA:	

I will, Master.
(They exit)

KANVA:	O trees of the ashram, who hide fairies in you:

She who would not drink until your roots were watered,
She who would not pluck your young sprouts in affection,
She who participated in your happy festival of blossoming,
She is going to her husband's; make your farewell calls
now.

(Listening to Cuckoo)

> *The trees of the forest, your relatives,*
> *Give you permission to leave,*
> *As if in response to my words,*
> *Through the soft voice of the cuckoo.*

DIVINE VOICE: *(Offstage)*

> *Resting by the beautiful lakes filled with pink lotuses,*
> *Protected from the rays of the hot sun by shady trees,*
> *And from the rising dust, blanketed by the soft pollen*
> *of lilies,*
> *May your path be gentle with peace-fairing winds!*

(Everyone listens with amazement.)

GAUTAMI: The fairies of the hermitage have spoken the words of farewell in affection. You must honor them.

SHAKUNTALA: *(Bows walking around, then aside)*
Priyamvada, though I am eager to see my husband, as I am getting ready to leave this ashram, my steps barely move forward.

PRIYAMVADA: You are not the only one to feel sad, Shakuntala. Look at the state of the grove itself, which is going to lose you.

> *The deer stopped grazing, the peacocks gave up dancing,*
> *As sallow leaves fall, the vines seem to weep.*

SHAKUNTALA: *(Remembering)*
Father, I must say good bye to my sister vine the "forest-flame".

KANVA: I know about your sibling affection for it. It is there to your right.

SHAKUNTALA: *(Embracing the creeper)*
"Forest-flame", embrace me with your branches. From now on I will be away from you.

KANVA: *My first wish was to find you a suitable husband.*

Now that you got that on your own effort,
I will have no worries except to see that this vine
Is united to this mango tree, its sweetheart.

Now get ready to leave.

SHAKUNTALA: *(To her friends)*
I leave her in your care.

BOTH
FRIENDS: To whose care you offer us?
(They weep)

KANVA: Anasuya, please do not cry. Instead, you must be giving courage to Shakuntala.
(They all walk on.)

SHAKUNTALA: Father, that deer grazing near the hut is pregnant. When she delivers, you should send someone to tell me the good news. Do not forget.

KANVA: I will not forget it, my daughter.

SHAKUNTALA: *(Pausing)*
Who is tugging at my dress?
(She turns around.)

KANVA: *It is the deer, whom you healed with Ingudi oil,*
When it cut its face with a sharp blade of grass,
And whom you fed with the wild mullet.
Like an adopted son, he does not want to let you go.

SHAKUNTALA: Why do you follow me so affectionately? Your mother died and you must learn to grow without her. Even without me, you have Father Kanva to care for you.
(She moves forward, weeping)

KANVA: *You shall have to check bravely the tears*
That flow to blur the vision of your eyes,
If you don't watch for the bumps and potholes

Of your path, your feet will come to grief.

SARANGARAVA:

I heard that relatives must go back at the edge of waters. Here is the edge of the lake. Here you should instruct us and go back.

KANVA:

In that case, let us stand here under the shade of this fig tree.

(They all do so.)

KANVA:

(To himself)

What fitting message could I send to King Dushyanta?

(He reflects)

SHAKUNTALA: *(Aside to Anasuya)*

Look! His mate being hidden from his view by the lotus leaves, the Chakravaka bird cries anxiously. It is very saddening.

ANASUYA:

I think so too.

Without lover beside, the nights pass slowly,
Yet hope forces us to bear the pain of separation.

KANVA:

Sarangarava, when you present Shakuntala to King Dushyanta, address him with these words in my name.

SARANGARAVA:

As you command, Master.

KANVA:

Remember that I am a hermit and think of your heritage,
And the love she has showered on you on her own,
Look upon her as an equal among your wives,
Rest lies with the fate; we could ask nothing else.

SARANGARAVA:

I have the message, Master.

KANVA: Shakuntala, I must advise you now. Though I live
                in a forest, I do know something of the world.

SARANGARAVA:

                Nothing lies outside the scope of the wise!

KANVA: When you reach your husband's house,
                Serve your elders; treat the fellow wives as dear friends.
                When your husband shows anger at you, do not cross him,
                Be kind to your servants; do not become vain with the
                wealth.
                That is how girls become good wives; others bring grief.

                What is your opinion, Gautami?

GAUTAMI: A bride needs no other advice. Daughter, do
                remember these words.

KANVA: You may now embrace your friends and me.

SHAKUNTALA: Father, Anasuya and Priyamvada are not coming
                with me?

KANVA: I must think of getting them married too. So it
                would not be appropriate to send them with you.
                But Gautami will accompany you.

SHAKUNTALA: *(Embracing Father Kanva)*
                How will I ever manage, torn from the father's
                breast, uprooted like a sandalwood vine from the
                hills?

KANVA: Why are you so afraid, daughter?
                You are a wife of an illustrious husband,
                When engrossed in tasks such a position brings,
                When you bear him a son, like the east brings light,
                Your pain of separation from me will disappear.

                (Shakuntala falls at his feet in homage.)
                May all that I wish for you happen!

SHAKUNTALA: *(Approaching Priyamvada and Anasuya.)*

Embrace me together, my dear friends.

BOTH FRIENDS:

(Doing so)

Shakuntala, if the king hesitates in recognizing you, show him the ring engraved with his name.

SHAKUNTALA: At such thought of suspicion my heart trembles.

BOTH
FRIENDS: Don't be afraid. Our deep love for you is suspicious of the worst.

SARANGARAVA:

The sun has risen high. Sister, we must go.

SHAKUNTALA: *(Facing the ashram)*

Would I ever see this ashram again, Father?

KANVA: Listen—

When you become the wife of the ruler of this wide earth,
And bear Dushyanta a son unrivaled in valor,
He would hand his son the burden of kingdom
And shall retire with you to this ashram.

GAUTAMI: It's getting very late. Shakuntala, let your father turn back. No, you will not do that. Sir, we must go.

KANVA: Daughter, I must attend to my duties of the ashram.

SHAKUNTALA: *(Embracing him again)*

The meditation has thinned your body. Do not worsen it over me.

KANVA: *(Sighing)*

How can grief weaken me when I see the grains,
You scattered as offering, germinate at the cottage door!

Go now. God be with you on your journey.
(Shakuntala and the escorting group leave.)

BOTH FRIENDS:

(Looking at Shakuntala)

O dear! She is lost to the forest.

KANVA: *(Sighing)*

Anasuya, You friend is gone. Hold your grief and follow me home.

(All turn around to go home.)

BOTH FRIENDS:

Father, without Shakuntala, the ashram looks empty as we enter.

KANVA: It is your affection that makes it so.

(Walking, thinking)

Now that I have sent away Shakuntala to her husband's house, I feel relieved.

A daughter is someone else's possession.
Having sent my daughter to her husband
I resume certain tranquility of mind,
As if what is given for safekeeping is discharged.

(All Exit)

CURTAIN

Act V

(On the stage are seen Dushyanta and the court jester seated.)

COURT JESTER:

(Listening)
Listen to the song accompanied by tonally pure music coming from your music room. It must be the queen, Hamsavati, practicing music.

DUSHYANTA: Be quiet while I listen to it.
(A song is heard offstage.)
When you longed for the nectar of flowers,
How eagerly mango blossoms embraced you!
Because now you dwell within the lotuses,
O bee, have you forgotten the former love?

DUSHYANTA: What a sensuous song!
COURT JESTER:

Did you get the hidden meaning of the song?
DUSHYANTA: (Smiling)
I do know the implication. I used to be very dear to her once. Now it is an issue of reproach for showing my love to the other queens. Madhavya, go and tell her as my words that she had succeeded in her intention.

COURT JESTER:

As you command, My Lord.

(He gets up.)
But, you are engaging an inept hand to grab the
bear by hair. I will have as much luck as a passionless ascetic will.

DUSHYANTA: Go. You are a man of the world; you can manage.
COURT JESTER:

What other choice?
(He leaves.)

DUSHYANTA: Her song gives me this strong feel of yearning,
though I do not miss any one. Perhaps,
Even a happy man, when he sees beautiful sights
Or hears sweet sounds, is filled with a longing,
As if he recalls in his mind, with out his knowledge,
Deep-embedded and fond relationships of his past lives.

(He seems pre-occupied.)
(The chamberlain enters.)

CHAMBERLAIN:

How old I have become!
I have taken this service as a custom
When the king asked me to be at the palace.
Many years have gone by me.
Now I need this cane even to stand.

What business must I inform of My Lord? Ooh!
Anyway, I am not so enthused to inform him of the
arrival of the pupils of Kanva, when he has just
risen from the seat of Justice. But then the rulers
cannot rest. Because,
The sun never unyokes his horses,
The wind blows day and night,
The Sesha ever bears the burden of the earth,
That's the state of people with such duties.

I am engaged for one such.
(Walking about, and looking)
There is My Lord.
After attending to people's needs like a father,
He is peacefully enjoying his solitude,
Like the lord of elephants, having sent them
To the pasture, shelters from the heat of the sun.

(Approaching the king)
Be victorious, My Lord. Some hermits from the ashram in the foothills of the Himalayas are here to see you. Some women accompany them. They have a message from Father Kanva. I await My Lord's command.

DUSHYANTA: *(In surprise)*
Ladies with a message from Father Kanva?

CHAMBERLAIN:
Yes, My Lord.

DUSHYANTA: In that case, tell our chaplain Somarata to receive them with the proper ceremony and ask him to accompany them to me. I await them in the place proper for them.

CHAMBERLAIN:
As you command, My Lord.
(He exits)

DUSHYANTA: *(Getting up)*
Vetravati, lead me to the Fire Sanctuary.

FEMALE GUARD:
This way, My Lord.
(She leads him)

DUSHYANTA: *(Taking an authoritative posture)*

Most people are happy to get what they wanted.
But a king must worry with every achievement.
Because,
It is easier to get what one desires
Than to protect that which one has.
Kingship is more weariness than rest,
Like an umbrella held by one's own hand.

BARDS: (*Offstage*)
                Hail to you, My Lord.

FIRST VOICE: *With no thought to your comfort,*
                For the welfare of your subjects,
                You exhaust yourself every day.
                Such is your good nature
                Like the tree that bears intense heat
                At the top to dissipate its severity
                And offer coolness under its branches
                To all who seek shelter.

SECOND VOICE:

You discipline the wayward by punishment
You resolve our conflicts and save us in hard times.
One finds many friends in prosperity,
But you are a kinsman always to all your people.

DUSHYANTA: This in deed refreshes the tired mind.
                (He moves on)

FEMALE GUARD:

Here are the steps to the Fire Sanctuary, My Lord.
It has been cleaned recently and the holy cow
stands near by for the fresh milk for oblation. Please
go up the steps.

DUSHYANTA: *(Ascends the steps, and pauses, putting his right hand on the attendant's shoulder.)*
Vetravati, I wonder why Father Kanva sent these hermits!
Have the austerities of the sages been hindered?
Did someone violate the creatures of the ashram?
Did my misdeeds cause the trees to become barren?
With these many possible thoughts, my mind is torn.

FEMALE GUARD:
My Lord, I think, because of your good character, they have come to bestow their blessings upon you.
(Enter Shakuntala with Mother Gautami, behind Sarangarava and Saradvata escorted by the Chamberlain and the Chaplain.)

CHAMBERLAIN:
This way, sirs.

SARANGARAVA:
Saradvata,
Be mighty the king and steadfast in his duty;
Be that even his meanest subjects are righteous;
Yet, with my mind used to perpetual solitude,
I feel as if I am on fire, when I see all these palace people!

SARADVATA: It is all right to feel that way on entering the city. I feel the same.
A wakeful person looks at a sleeper
As a clean person would at a unclean;
And I look at these men
As a free man would at a man in bondage.

SHAKUNTALA: *(Observing an omen)*
Mother, my right eye splutters an ill omen.

GAUTAMI: Daughter, kill the omen. Your husband will give
                  you only happiness.
                  (They walk towards the king.)
CHAPLAIN: *(Pointing at the king)*
                  O hermits, there stands the king, the protector of
                  all—regardless of the caste or creed—to receive
                  you. Look at him.
SARANGARAVA:
                  We appreciate his courtesy. I understand this, because:
                  Trees bend low with their fruits,
                  The clouds with the water they bear,
                  Good man is humble in his wealth,
                  Such is the nature of an altruist.

FEMALE GUARD:
                  My Lord, they look happy. I think they have good
                  news to tell you.
DUSHYANTA: *(Looks at Shakuntala)*
                  Who is that lady wearing the veil
                  That obscures her lovely figure?
                  She stands among the ascetics
                  Like a bud amidst sallow leaves.

FEMALE GUARD:
                  I could not answer to your curiosity, My Lord. But
                  she does look lovely.
DUSHYANTA: Well, one should not describe other's wife so.
SHAKUNTALA: *(Touching her heart, to herself)*
                  My heart, why do you tremble so? Remember his
                  devotion for me and be courageous.
CHAPLAIN: *(Goes towards the king)*

| | Here are the hermits received with the proper rites. They bring a message from their master, Father Kanva. |

DUSHYANTA: I shall listen.

HERMITS: *(Raising their right hands in benediction)*
Be victorious, O King.

DUSHYANTA: I salute you all.

HERMITS: May your desires be fulfilled!

DUSHYANTA: Do the ashram rites remain undisturbed, O hermits?

HERMITS: *How could they be disturbed when you rule?*
How could darkness remain when the sun shines?

DUSHYANTA: Those words give me a purpose to be a king? The reverend Kanva, is he in good health?

SARANGARAVA:
People with spiritual control are always well. He asks me to inquire of your health before I tell you his message.

DUSHYANTA: What is his command?

SARANGARAVA:
I approve of the mutual marriage between you and my daughter. As:
You are the best to be cherished of the mankind,
And Shakuntala, the best embodiment of womanhood;
In uniting the couple of equal individual merit
The creator has acted finally with no fault.

Now that she is pregnant with your child, keep her in holy matrimony.

GAUTAMI: Sir, What else could I say except that I have nothing to add. Since,
Neither she consulted her guardian,
Nor you asked for the permission from her relatives,

> *So to what has been decided between you,*
> *What else we could say at all?*

SHAKUNTALA: *(To herself)*
How is My Lord going to respond now?

DUSHYANTA: What are you saying?

SHAKUNTALA: *(To herself)*
How cold his voice sounds!

SARANGARAVA:
What are we saying? You know better the way of the world.
> *If a wife lives at home away from her husband,*
> *Though blameless, people would suspect her.*
> *Hence the relatives ask her to stay at the house*
> *Of her husband, whether there is love or not.*

DUSHYANTA: Did I marry her?

SHAKUNTALA: *(To herself, with sorrow)*
My suspects become true!

SARANGARAVA:
Can you turn away from the duty, just because you dislike your action now?

DUSHYANTA: Why do you ask me such presumptuous questions?

SARANGARAVA:
Such aberrant behavior is to be seen in men drunk with power.

DUSHYANTA: You insult me gravely.

GAUTAMI: *(To Shakuntala)*
Daughter, do not be shy. Take your veil off. Perhaps then, your husband would recognize you.
(Shakuntala does so.)

DUSHYANTA: *(Fixes his gaze upon her and to himself)*
I am offered a flawless beauty,

Not knowing whether she was once mine,
I feel like the bee trapped at dawn in jasmine:
It could neither enjoy nor leave the flower.

(He continues to reflect.)

FEMALE
GUARD: My Lord is a righteous man. Finding such a beau-
            tiful lady, who else would hesitate?

SARANGARAVA:

            My Lord, why are you silent?

DUSHYANTA: O hermit, however hard I think I do not seem to
            remember marrying her. In such a case, how can I
            accept a pregnant lady without condemning myself
            in my own eyes as an adulterer?

SHAKUNTALA:*(To herself)*
            He doubts the marriage itself. All my hopes desert
            me now.

SARANGARAVA:

            Not so.
            Approving your seduction of his daughter,
            He honors you by presenting her to you.
            But would a thief be absolved of his crime,
            Simply by presenting him with what he stole?

SARADVATA: Sarangarava, stop. Enough is said. Shakuntala, we
            have said what we should. You heard the king. You
            reply to his words.

SHAKUNTALA: *(To herself)*
            When love has sidestepped, what use to remind
            him of it? But, for my own good, I must do some-
            thing.
            (Aloud)
            My husband,

(She falters and speaks to herself)
When he suspects my right to call him so, how could I?
(Aloud)
O, Puru, is it right in your opinion to reject me when you made promises and cherished me as I opened my heart to you at the ashram?

DUSHYANTA: *(Covering his ears)*
Stop the blasphemy.
You slander my name and yours
In your sullen mood
Like a river whose waves break endlessly
Eroding the beach trees and soiling its own waters.

SHAKUNTALA: If you hesitate because you believe I am someone else's wife, this gift may remove your doubt.

DUSHYANTA: That would be an example for evidence.

SHAKUNTALA: *(Feeling her finger for the ring)*
Oh, no! Oh, no! My finger is bare.
(She looks at Gautami with sadness.)

GAUTAMI: Daughter, while you were offering your worship at the river Ganges, it might have slipped off your hand.

DUSHYANTA: *(Smiling)*
This is in deed an example of female quick wit.

SHAKUNTALA: Fate has intervened here. But I can tell you something else.

DUSHYANTA: Now verbal accounts?

SHAKUNTALA: One day in the jasmine bower, you were sitting with me holding a lotus leaf filled with water...

DUSHYANTA: I am listening.

SHAKUNTALA: At that moment, Dhirgapangha, my adopted fawn came over there. You took pity and offered him water. But he would not come near and drink from your hand because you were a stranger. When I gave him the water, he drank it immediately. Then you laughed and said that we all trust those who smell the same. You both belong to the forest.

DUSHYANTA: Such is the guile of female persuasion to lure the susceptible.

GAUTAMI: My Lord, you have no right to think so. She belongs to an ashram and therefore ignorant of such deceit.

DUSHYANTA: Venerable Mother,
Cunning is natural to female species.
It is so even in animals, let alone human species!
Until her young ones are hatched and ready to fly away
It is said that the cuckoo gets others to nurture them.

SHAKUNTALA: *(In anger)*
Brute, you look at others with your selfish heart. You put on a deceitful cover of virtue like a well covered over with grass.

DUSHYANTA: *(To himself)*
My doubtful mind is thrown into confusion with her genuine anger.
To my ruthlessness in not remembering her,
To my refusal to proclaim to a secret love,
Her eyebrows react, curving with grace,
As if in anger a bow is being snapped.

(Aloud)
Dushyanta's conduct is well known. Such statements do not match his character.

SHAKUNTALA: So I have become a harlot now, for giving myself into the hands of a sweet-mouthed, poison-hearted man of Puru dynasty.
(She covers her face with the edge of her dress and weeps.)

SARANGARAVA:

This is the inevitable result of unbridled passion.
One should therefore show caution
Especially in matters of secret liaisons,
Without knowing each other's heart,
As in this case, love may turn into hate.

DUSHYANTA: Why do you rely on her and throw accusations at me?

SARANGARAVA:

(Scornfully)
So it should be the other way around?
From the birth she has not been taught a deceit,
Her words are to be considered lies?
And he who practices deception
Like a science must be trusted!

DUSHYANTA: O Trustworthy, let us suppose I am deceitful. What would I gain with it?

SARANGARAVA:

Your destruction!

DUSHYANTA: It is unheard that Purus would pray for their destruction.

SARADVATA: Sarangarava, that is enough with the questions and answers. We have done what Father Kanva asked us to do.
(To the king)
There is your wife, accept or reject her.

As a husband, you are free to choose.

Lead the way, Gautami.
(They start to leave.)

SHAKUNTALA: He has rejected me. You too abandon me?
(She follows.)

GAUTAMI: *(Stopping)*
Sarangarava, this poor girl is following us. What would my daughter, rejected by her husband, do now?

SARANGARAVA:
(In anger)
Progressive woman, show your self-will.
(Shakuntala trembles in fear.)
Shakuntala,
If what the king says is true,
Then you have disgraced your family.
If you are pure in your heart,
You will bear to live in servitude here.

Stay here. We shall be going.

DUSHYANTA: O hermits, why do you deceive her so?
With the moon bloom the lilies of the night,
With the sun awaken the lotuses of the day.
Those who have control over their conduct
Would never embrace another man's wife.

SARANGARAVA:
If some distraction made you forget her, then a righteous man cannot reject her.

DUSHYANTA: I shall ask the chaplain.
If there is doubt: whether I have forgotten,
Or she speaks falsely,
Should I reject my own wife?

Or sin by touching another man's wife?

CHAPLAIN: *(Reflecting)*
                   We could resolve it this way.

DUSHYANTA: Instruct me, sir.

CHAPLAIN: She stays here until the child is born. The sages
                   have predicted that your first born will rule this
                   earth. If she bears a child with the proper marks as
                   prophesied, take her into your household. If not,
                   she can go back to her father.

DUSHYANTA: I shall follow my chaplain's suggestion.

CHAPLAIN: Come with me, Shakuntala.

SHAKUNTALA: Mother earth, give me deliverance from this.
                   (She leaves sobbing, with the priest and others.)
                   (Dushyanta, still forgetful because of the curse, reflects
                   on Shakuntala.)
                   (Shouts offstage.)
                   It is a wonder. It is a wonder.

DUSHYANTA: *(Listening)*
                   What is happening?
                   (Enters the chaplain.)

CHAPLAIN: *(In amazement)*
                   Your Majesty, an extra-ordinary thing has happened.

DUSHYANTA: What happened?

PRIEST: As the hermits turned to go, the girl went toward
                   them, cursing her fate, weeping and clutching her
                   breast in despair.

DUSHYANTA: And then?

CHAPLAIN: *There arose from the pool of Nymphs*
                   A flash of white light
                   Shaped like a woman
                   That seized the girl up and vanished.

(All show amazement.)

DUSHYANTA: Sir, we have settled that issue. Why waste our time with speculations? Go and take rest.

CHAPLAIN: Be victorious.   *(He leaves.)*

DUSHYANTA: Vetravati, I am very tired. Take me to my bedroom.

FEMALE
GUARD: This way, My Lord.

DUSHYANTA: *(To himself)*

I do not recall my marriage to the hermit girl,
Whom I rejected just now.
Yet, there is such pain in my heart,
As if I could have done it.

CURTAIN

Act VI

Prelude

(Enter a police officer, with two guards leading a bound fisherman.)

GUARDS: *(Beating the bound man)*
You thief! Tell us where you got the royal signet ring.

FISHERMAN: *(Trembling in fear)*
Please, sirs. I did not steal anything.

FIRST GUARD: Taking you for a fine Brahmin, did the king present you with this?

FISHERMAN: Sir, I am a fisherman from the shores of Ganges.

SECOND GUARD:
Swine, did we ask your caste?

OFFICER: Suchaka, let him tell it in his own words. Do not interrupt him.

BOTH GUARDS:
Yes, sir.
(Looking at the fisherman)
Go on. Go on.

FISHERMAN: Sir, I support my family by fishing.

OFFICER: *(Laughing)*
A very clean profession, in deed!

FISHERMAN: Do not say that, sir.

It is said that a man born into a trade
Should not give it up however low it be,
Even the butcher though he slaughters
Animals may have the softest heart.

OFFICER: Go on.

FISHERMAN: One day, I netted a carp. When I cut its gut open, I
                found this gem-studded ring. I took it to the mar-
                ket to sell it and that's when they arrested me. Kill
                me or release me. That's the whole story, sir.

OFFICER: Januka, this ring without doubt smells as if it had
                been in the belly of a fish. We must find out how
                the ring showed up there. Let us go to the palace.

BOTH
GUARDS: Yes sir.
                (To the fisherman)
                You stink! Move on.
                (They take a few steps.)

OFFICER: Suchaka, stand guard at this main gate. I will
                inform His Majesty of how we came into the pos-
                session of the ring, and ask him for his decree.

BOTH
GUARDS: Go in for the king's favor.
                (The police officer leaves.)

SUCHAKA: *(To the second Guard)*
                Januka, he is taking a long time.

JANUKA: You have to approach the king at the right time.

SUCHAKA: My hands are itching to chop this swine's head.
                (He points to the fisherman.)

FISHERMAN: It is a sin to kill someone for no reason.

JANUKA: Here comes our chief with the royal decree in his
                hand.

	(To the fisherman)
	Looks like you will be either offered to the vultures or to the dogs.
OFFICER:	*(Entering)*
	Release him. His account of finding the ring is agreeable to the king.
SUCHAKA:	Just as you say, sir.
JANUKA:	He comes back from the gates of Death.
	(He unties the fisherman.)
FISHERMAN:	*(Bowing)*
	Sir, what do I do for today's living?
OFFICER:	Here, the king was kind enough to reward you with gold, equivalent to the value of the ring.
	(He throws the gold at him.)
FISHERMAN:	*(Prostrating at his feet)*
	I am in deed blessed.
SUCHAKA:	Yes, the king blesses him with his life and sets him on an elephant.
JANUKA:	This reward shows that the ring must be worth a great deal.
OFFICER:	I do not think it is because of the gems. Just seeing it reminded His Majesty of someone very dear to him. For a moment, though he was by nature calm and serious, there were tears in his eyes.
SUCHAKA:	Then, the king is pleased at you.
JANUKA:	Not at us. But at this killer of fish.
	(He points to the fisherman, enviously.)
FISHERMAN:	Take half of this for your drinks, sirs.
JANUKA:	That is admirable!
OFFICER:	Suddenly, you have become my friend. Let us go and toast to this friendship forever. Let us go and celebrate.

(They all leave.)

(The end of the prelude)

(Enters SANUMATI, a nymph, flying through the air.)

SANUMATI: I have accomplished my task at the pool of
             Nymphs. The hermits have finished their obla-
             tional bath. Now, I will observe the state of affairs
             with the king. Because of my association with her
             mother Menaka, Shakuntala is like my family.
             Menaka asked me to look after her daughter.
             (She looks around)
             Though it is time for the spring festival, the palace
             seems gloomy without celebrations. I could find out
             everything by concentrating on my powers. But, I
             must respect others' privacy. So, I will make myself
             invisible and stay beside those two maids to gather
             what I can from them.
             (She descends dancing.)
             *(Enter a maid, looking at the mango sprouts and
             another maid behind her.)*

FIRST MAID: *In red, green and yellow colors of lively spring,*
             The mango sprouts mark the start of the festival.

SECOND MAID:

             What are you mumbling to yourself, Parabhritika
             (Cuckoo)?

FIRST MAID: Madhukarika (Little Bee), Cuckoo is excited at the
             sight of the mango blossoms.

MADHUKARIKA:

             (Catching her pun, delightedly)
             What? Is spring here already?

PARABHRITIKA:

> Yes, Madhukarika. It is time for you to buzz with intoxication.

MADHUKARIKA:

> Hold me, Parabhritika, while I stand on my toes to break a twig of mango blossoms to offer to the god of Love.

PARABHRITIKA:

> Only if I get half the outcome of your worship.

MADHUKARIKA:

> Of course, that goes without saying. Because, though we have two bodies, our life is one.
>
> *(Thus, supported by her friend, she breaks a twig of mango sprouts.)*
>
> Although, the buds are still unopened, they smell sweet as I break them from the branch.
>
> *(She joins her hands in prayer.)*
>
> *I offer this twig of mango blossoms*
> *To Cupid bearing the bow, to be an arrow*
> *To excel his five for the benefit of women*
> *Whose husbands are away on travels!*
>
> *(She throws the twig into the air.)*
> *(The chamberlain enters, showing exasperation.)*

CHAMBERLAIN:

> Stop that. When the king has prohibited by order the Spring Festival, you break twigs of mango blossoms?

BOTH MAIDSERVANTS:

> *(Showing fear)*
> Please forgive us. We did not know.

CHAMBERLAIN:

You did not know what the king has ordered? Even the spring trees and their dependent creepers seem to have obeyed his command. Look!

Mango buds, though blossomed, are devoid of pollen,
The amaranth has long put out buds, yet they remain so,
The song of cuckoo is stifled, though winter is long gone,
Cupid's arrow half-drawn from the quiver stays still.

SANUMATI: No doubt. The king has great powers.

PARABHRITIKA:

Sir, we came only a few days ago sent by our queen's brother Mitravasu. We were given this pleasure garden to look after. That is why we did not know of this account until now.

CHAMBERLAIN:

Well, do not do it again.

BOTH MAIDSERVANTS:

Sir, we are curious now. If it is all right for people like us to know, please tell us why the king had prohibited the Spring Festival.

SANUMATI:

People love these festivals. There must be a strong reason against the Festival.

CHAMBERLAIN:

It is known to many now. I do not see any reason not to tell you. You must have heard the story of Shakuntala's rejection.

BOTH MAIDSERVANTS:

Yes, sir, from the king's brother-in-law, we heard up to the showing up of the ring.

CHAMBERLAIN:

> Then, there is not much to tell you. When His
> Majesty saw the ring, he remembered that he had
> in deed married her in secret. And he is now filled
> with the remorse for rejecting her. Therefore,
> *He looks at pleasures in disgust and refuses*
> *To be waited upon by his ministers;*
> *He spends his nights sleepless*
> *Tossing about restlessly in bed.*
> *When he offers some charming words*
> *To the women of the palace,*
> *They die flat, with slips of their names,*
> *And he is filled with embarrassment.*

SANUMATI: Dear me!

CHAMBERLAIN:

> Because of his state of mind, the Festival has been
> prohibited.

BOTH MAIDSERVANTS:

> We understand.
> *(They leave.)*
> *(Enter King, looking depressed, with the court jester*
> *and the female guard.)*

CHAMBERLAIN:

> *(Looking at the king)*
> How wonderful people of handsome features look
> in every state of mind! Though he is filled with sor-
> row, His Majesty looks lovely.
> *Devoid of special ornaments, on his left arm*
> *Only a loose golden bracelet, his lips laden with sighs,*
> *His eyes wakeful with sadness, he looks brilliant*
> *Like a polished diamond, though thinned in the cut.*

SANUMATI: *(Looking at Dushyanta)*
                     No wonder Shakuntala loves him still, even though
                     he has rejected her.

DUSHYANTA: *(Deep in thought, walking about)*
                     Once my dear tried to wake my sleeping heart in vain.
                     Now it is all awake tortured with the painful sorrow.

SANUMATI: Such is the fate of the hermit girl!

COURT JESTER:
                     (To himself)
                     Another attack of Shakuntala sickness! Is there any
                     cure for it?

CHAMBERLAIN:
                     (Approaching the king)
                     Be victorious, My Lord! I have inspected the pleas-
                     ure garden. My Lord may visit it for pleasure at
                     your convenience.

DUSHYANTA: Vetravati, tell Minister Pisuna as my words that I
                     am a little indisposed because of sleeplessness and
                     he should take the chair of Justice today. Any deed
                     concerning the citizens that he looks into, he may
                     write it down and send it for my attention.

FEMALE GUARD:
                     Yes, My Majesty.
                     (She exits.)

DUSHYANTA: Vatayana, You are free to go too.

CHAMBERLAIN:
                     Certainly, Your Majesty.
                     (He leaves)

COURT JESTER:
                     The flies are gotten rid of. Now you can relax in the
                     pleasure garden, which is very pleasant since the
                     winter is gone.

DUSHYANTA: It is in deed true of what people say that misfortunes strike at your weak spots. Because:
As soon as the darkness that besieged my heart
Vanished by the restored memory of my dear,
The god of Love, as if laying in wait for me,
Shoots me with his bow the mango blossom[3].

COURT JESTER:
Stay there. I will destroy the cupid's arrow with this stick.
(He raises his staff to bring down the mango buds.)
DUSHYANTA: *(Smiling)*
All right. I have seen the power of Brahmins. Tell me where I could sit, and relax when all these creepers remind me of the beauty of Shakuntala.

COURT JESTER:
You ordered Chaturika to have the sketch of Shakuntala, which you painted, brought to you in the spring belvedere. Let us go there.
DUSHYANTA: That's how I must comfort my heart. Lead the way.
COURT JESTER:
This way, My Lord.
(They walk about; Sanumati follows them.)
The spring belvedere with its white marble seat seems to invite you for quiet meditation. Let us sit down, My Lord.
(They both enter the belvedere and sit down.)
SANUMATI: *(To herself)*

---

3. Mango blossom is supposedly one of Cupid's five arrows.

I will hide behind these creepers and see the picture of my friend. That way I can tell Shakuntala of her husband's affection.

DUSHYANTA: Friend, now I remember everything of our first encounter. I told you all that. You were absent when I refused her. Even so, you never brought her name before me. I suppose, you too had forgotten her.

COURT JESTER:

No, I had not forgotten. After you told me everything, you also mentioned laughingly that it was all a game and I should not take it seriously. I, with my dull-witted mind, accepted it. It came to pass thus because the fate is powerful.

SANUMATI: *(To herself)*
Yes, indeed.

DUSHYANTA: *(Reflecting)*
Help me, my friend!

COURT JESTER:

Collect your self, My Lord! It does not suit you. Good men would not yield to grief. Mountains are not shaken even by strong winds.

DUSHYANTA:

When I recollect her state of mind after I rejected her, I tremble with guilt.
Rejected by me, she tries to follow her relatives,
But, the pupil of Kanva halts her.
Once again she turns to look at me with her tearful eyes.
Cruel me, it burns in me like a poisoned dart.

SANUMATI: He is self-righteous and is rightfully so distressed.

COURT JESTER:

My deduction is that a heavenly being must have carried her off.

DUSHYANTA: Who else would dare to touch such a faithful wife!
             Her friends told me that her mother was the
             nymph Menaka. I suspect either Menaka or her
             friends must have carried Shakuntala away.

SANUMATI: It would be a wonder if he comes under delusion!

COURT JESTER:
             In that case, union is just a matter of time.

DUSHYANTA: How?

COURT JESTER:
             No parents would like to see their daughter
             unhappy, separated for long from her husband.

DUSHYANTA: *Whether it was a dream, or an illusion, or a mental*
             disease,
             Or the end of the cumulated fruits of my good deeds,
             It is now for sure gone without recompense to recovery
             As if the desire of my heart bounced off a steep cliff!

COURT JESTER:
             Not at all. The ring itself is an example of how
             unimaginable unions could take place.

DUSHYANTA: *(Looking at the ring)*
             How unfortunate you are to fall from the place dif-
             ficult to reach!
             Your fate, like mine, poor ring,
             Reflects a lack of the fruits of good deeds.
             You won a place among the fingers with lovely red nails,
             But only to slip away from such a favor.

SANUMATI: It would have been unbecoming on someone else's
             finger.

COURT JESTER:
             What prompted you to give this signet ring to her
             to wear?

SANUMATI: That is what I am curious to know.

DUSHYANTA: Listen. When I was leaving for the city, she asked
me with tears how long would it be before she could
see me.

COURT JESTER:

And then...

DUSHYANTA: I put this ring on her hand with these words:
Read every day one letter of my name
On this ring until you reach the end,
By then, some one would come, my dear,
To escort you to the palace of my desire.

My cruel heart in distraction failed to fulfill that
promise!

SANUMATI: A romantic gesture ruined by the fate!

COURT JESTER:

How did it get into the entrails of the carp like a
hook?

DUSHYANTA: At the Sachi ford of Ganges, when she was offering
water in worship, it slipped off her finger.

COURT JESTER:

Yes, it is possible.

SANUMATI: That is why a righteous king like Dushyanta had
doubts about his marriage to the hermit girl
Shakuntala. But then, the strong feeling of love
such as what he shows cannot be forgotten. What is
this all about?

DUSHYANTA: The blame is on the ring.

COURT JESTER:

(To himself)

Madness would take hold of him.

DUSHYANTA: *Why did you leave the soft and supple finger*

Of her hand and sink low into the water?

Because,
Mindless objects cannot notice merit.
But, how could have I not seen my love?

COURT JESTER:

(To himself)
I will be eaten alive by hunger.

DUSHYANTA: Dear, now that my heart suffers with the remorse
for rejecting you for no reason, won't you take pity
on me and show yourself again?
(Chaturika enters carrying a painting.)

CHATURIKA: My Lord, here is the painting of your queen.
(She shows him the picture.)

COURT JESTER:

(Looking at it)
Very beautiful indeed! Delightful picture redolent
with passionate feeling. My sight stumbles at the
high and low curves.

SANUMATI: O dear, the king is indeed a talented artist. She
looks as if she is in front of me.

DUSHYANTA: *Though the portrait suffers my ill talent,*
The outline of her beauty shines through!

SANUMATI: It is a statement of affection mixed with genuine
contrition.

COURT JESTER:

I see three figures here. They are all beautiful.
Which one is your Shakuntala?

DUSHYANTA: Which one do you think?

COURT JESTER:

I think this one with the flowers falling from her
loosely bound hair, drops of sweat on her face, with

slender drooping arms, and loosely tied dress, looking somewhat tired, standing against the vine that winds around the mango tree. The others are her friends.

DUSHYANTA: You are clever. I have left marks of my feeling there.

Around the edges where my fingers pressed,
You see a streak of dirty smudge.
Here the paint swells to reveal
The spot where my tear fell!

Chaturika, the background is only half-painted. Go and get me some brushes.

CHATURIKA: Sir, Madhavya, would you please hold this painting while I am gone.

DUSHYANTA: I will hold it.

(He does so.)
(Maid exits)
(With a sigh, the king continues)
I rejected her when she was in the flesh before me,
Now I yearn for her when she is a mere picture.
When the streaming river was in my path,
I ignored it and now I thirst for a mirage.

COURT JESTER:

(To himself)
True river then, now a mirage!
(Aloud)
What else do you intend to paint, My Lord?

SANUMATI: Perhaps he wants to paint the places she liked very much.

DUSHYANTA: Well,

A pair of swans on the sandy banks of flowing Malini,
On the sides, resting stags in the foothills of Himalayas,
Under the tree where the bark garments are hung to dry,

I want to show a doe rubbing her left eye on a buckhorn.

COURT JESTER:

(To himself)
The way I see it, he should fill the painting with the long-bearded hermits.

DUSHYANTA: There is something else too. I forgot to paint Shakuntala's favorite object.

COURT JESTER:

What is it?

SANUMATI: It must be something a young hermit girl would wear, I suppose.

DUSHYANTA: *I haven't done the Sirisha flower in her hair,*
The stalk behind her ear, petals against the cheeks,
And, the necklace of lotus stalks, soothing and soft
As the autumn moon, resting between her breasts.

COURT JESTER:

Why does she stand there, covering her face with her sanguine-colored fingers, as if frightened?
(Looking at the picture closely)
Ah! There is the rascal bee, intoxicated with the nectar of flowers, buzzing about on her face.

DUSHYANTA: Stop the villain then!

COURT JESTER:

You are the one who should be punishing the culprit for misconduct.

DUSHYANTA: I shall. O guest of the flowers, why do you hover and bother her?
On the petals of the flower
Waits the female bee, your love.
Though she is thirsty for the nectar
She would not relish it without you.

SANUMATI: A good reason to ward him off!
COURT JESTER:
               Some species could be very stubborn.
DUSHYANTA:
               You ignore a royal command! Listen then:
               Lovely as the virgin blossoms of a young tree,
               My beloved's lips, which I drank during love,
               If you ever dare to bite those red lips, O bee,
               I will have you imprisoned inside a lotus.

COURT JESTER:
               Who would not be scared by such severe punishment?
               (Laughing, to himself)
               He is so mad that by association I would become one.
               (Aloud)
               It's just a painting, My Lord.
DUSHYANTA: Just a painting?
SANUMATI: Even I felt otherwise. Why should it not delude the
               painter?
DUSHYANTA: Thank you for being so damn realistic.
               My heart was filled with a renewed joy
               As if I was seeing her in the flesh to my wish;
               You awoke me from my sweet memories
               To turn her back into picture that she was.

               (He drops a tear.)
SANUMATI: His present behavior of yearning contradicts his
               past conduct.
DUSHYANTA: There seems no respite from unhappiness I feel, my
               friend.
               My sleeplessness robs me
               From dreaming of union with her;

And, my tearful eyes prevent me
From looking at her in the picture.

SANUMATI: Good, Good. I have seen enough of atonement from you for the cause of Shakuntala.

(Enter Chaturika)

CHATURIKA: My Lord, as I was coming back with the paint box....

DUSHYANTA: And?

CHATURIKA: The second queen Vasumati, accompanied by Taralika, snatched it from my hands and said that she herself would bring it to Your Majesty.

COURT JESTER:

How did you get away from her?

CHATURIKA: Her Majesty's dress was caught on a branch. While Taralika was freeing it, I removed myself swiftly.

DUSHYANTA: Mathavya, she is very proud of my regard for her. You must protect this picture from her.

COURT JESTER:

Protect you, you mean.

(He takes the painting and stands up.)

If you succeed in freeing yourself from the palace ladies, you can come and call on me in the Cloud Tower.

(He rushes off.)

SANUMATI: Though the king's heart is elsewhere, still he is considerate to his former loves. So his affection is permanent.

(Enter a female guard with a scroll.)

VETRAVATI: Victory to My Lord.

DUSHYANTA: Did you happen to see the queen Vasumati coming this way, Vetravati?

VETRAVATI: I did, My Lord. But when she saw me with the scroll, she turned back.

DUSHYANTA: Her Majesty is thoughtful not to interfere in my duties.

VETRAVATI: The minister had asked me to report to you that since he had so many revenue issues to look into, he could attend to only one citizen's case. He had put down the details of the case on this scroll for your personal attention.

DUSHYANTA: Let me see the scroll.

(She offers the scroll to the king.)

DUSHYANTA: *(Reads it)*

An overseas merchant called Dhanamitra has died in a shipwreck. Since he does not have any children, the wealth passes on to the King's treasury. So our minister writes. It is hard to have no children. Vetravati, since he is very rich, he might have had many wives. Find out if any one of his wives is pregnant.

VETRAVATI: My Lord, I heard that one of his wives, a daughter of a merchant, has recently solemnized the ritual of baby-shower.

DUSHYANTA: Then, the unborn child must inherit the wealth of the father. Go and tell this to the minister.

VETRAVATI: Yes, My Lord.

(She turns to go.)

DUSHYANTA: Just a minute.

VETRAVATI: I am here, My Lord.

DUSHYANTA: It does not matter whether one has offspring or not.
                Have it proclaimed henceforth
                That whenever my subjects
                Bereave the death of their loving relative,
                I shall personally look after them.

VETRAVATI:	I shall have it so proclaimed, My Lord.
	(Goes out and returns)
	My Lord, people welcomed your announcement like the rain due its season.
DUSHYANTA:	*(Sighing deeply)*
	Such is the reality. Without a proper offspring, the accumulated wealth finds its way into the hands of a stranger when the head of the family dies. That perhaps would be the case with the Puru dynasty when my end comes.
VETRAVATI:	Perish such evil thought!
DUSHYANTA:	Good came my way, but I spurned it.
SANUMATI:	Undoubtedly, he means Shakuntala when he deprecates himself
DUSHYANTA:	*I wed her to be my lawful wife,*
	And I dejected her after impregnating her with my race,
	Like deserting the earth, seasonally sown with seed,
	Before enjoying the bounty of its harvest.
SANUMATI:	Though you deserted her, your lineage will go on.
CHAMBERLAIN:	
	(Aside to Vetravati)
	The account of merchant's case had made Our Lord doubly miserable. Go and bring Madhavya who is resting in the Cloud Tower to console Our Lord.
VETRAVATI:	That would be good.
	(Vetravati goes out.)
DUSHYANTA:	Alas, the spirits of my ancestors would be alarmed of my situation!
	After me, without anyone in the family,
	They wonder who would do the rites of the Dead.
	Dejected with no offspring, the tears I shed

Form the pure water offering for them to drink.

(He faints.)

CHAMBERLAIN:

(Agitated)

Wake up, My Lord. Wake up!

SANUMATI: How terrible! Though there is light, the circumstances put the king in darkness. Shall I dispel his
darkness? But, I heard from the mother of
Mahendra, the Lord of the gods, when she was
comforting Shakuntala that in due time the gods
themselves would see to their union. Therefore I
should not waste my time here. In any case, I should
recount the events here to my friend Shakuntala.

(She rises up into the air and disappears.)

VOICE: *(Offstage)*

I am a Brahmin! I'm a Brahman!

DUSHYANTA: *(Recovering, and listening)*

That's Mathavya's cry for help. Where is he?

VETRAVATI: *(Enters in alarm.)*

Oh, My Lord, save Mathavya!

DUSHYANTA: What has happened?

VETRAVATI: Some invisible power has seized him from the
Cloud Tower and placed him on the highest point
of the dome.

DUSHYANTA: *(Rising)*

Do spirits dare to invade my own home? But then,

No one can vouch for the errors that result

From oversight in one's every day activities.

Even a king could not know all the actions

That his subjects would do in various ways.

OFF STAGE VOICE:

My Lord, help me! Help me!

DUSHYANTA: *(Walking briskly towards the direction of the voice)*

Dear friend, do not be afraid.

COURT JESTER'S VOICE:

(Offstage)

Do not be afraid? He got me by the neck and bent me in three places.

DUSHYANTA: *(Looking around)*

Get me my bow, quickly!

A GREEK SERVANT:

(Entering carrying weapons in her hand)

My Lord, here are the bow and arrows and your hand gloves.

(The king takes them.)

A VOICE: *(Offstage)*

Like a tiger, in search of fresh blood,

Grabs the throat of an animal, I hold you;

Let Dushyanta, who protects the timid

With his bow, save you from me!

DUSHYANTA: *(Angrily)*

Did he mock me? Stand there, you barbarian. Your end is near. *(Stringing his arrow)*

Vetravati, lead me to the staircase.

VETRAVATI: This way, My Lord.

(All walk in haste.)

DUSHYANTA: *(Looking around)*

There is no one here!

COURT JESTER'S VOICE:

(Offstage)

Help me. Help me. You cannot see me but I can see you. Hopes for my life are as slim as that of a mouse in the grips of a cat.

DUSHYANTA: You are arrogant with your power of invisibility. My arrow will find you. I am aiming my arrow at you.
It will kill you, the villain, and save the oppressed
Like swan that separates milk from its watery mixture!

(The king prepares to aim his arrow. Enter MATALI, carrying Madhavya.)

MATALI: Long live the king!
There are enough evil spirits for the target practice,
Those are the ones at whom your arrows should aim.
Great people shower upon their friends,
Kind and gentle glances not those cruel arrows.

DUSHYANTA: Matali! Welcome, O charioteer of Mahendra!

COURT JESTER:
He nearly killed me and you are happy to invite him!

MATALI: *(Smiling)*
Hear me, sir, why Mahendra, the Lord of the gods, had sent me here.

DUSHYANTA: I am listening.

MATALI: There is an army of demons under Durjaya, the offspring of Kalanemi.

DUSHYANTA: Yes, I heard of them. Narada told me of them.

MATALI: *Your friend Indra seeks your help to confront them,*
As it is in your destiny to meet them in battle.
The darkness that cannot be dispelled by the sun
Is swept away by the moon that rules the night.

And so mount the chariot of Mahendra, just as you are, armed with the bow and arrows, ready for the victory.

DUSHYANTA: Lord Mahendra honors me with such a request. But, why did you play this game on Mathavya?

MATALI: I will tell you. For some reason you seemed to be in distress. Therefore, I wanted to provoke anger in you.
Fiery coals glow when they are stirred,
Snake when provoked sneers with its hood,
Whoever has some spark of energy in them
Will glow warmly when aroused.

DUSHYANTA: *(Looking at Madhavya)*
I cannot disobey a command from the Lord of the gods. Therefore, inform the minister, Pisuna, of what happened here and give this message to him.
In the interim of my absence he shall rule my subjects,
As my stringed bow is engaged for another business.

COURT JESTER:
As you command, My Lord.
(He exits.)

MATALI: This way, Sir.

(All exit.)

CURTAIN

ACT VII

(Enter Matali and Dushyanta in flying chariot.)

DUSHYANTA: Matali, I have done my duty entrusted upon me by Lord Mahendra. However, I feel I do not deserve the honors that were showered upon me later.

MATALI: *(Smiling)*
Sir, both of you feel that the honors were unworthy.
You think the favor you have done Lord Mahendra
Does not deserve honors he bestowed on you.
And, he earnestly considers little such honors
For the enormous service you rendered him.

DUSHYANTA: Well, Matali, I do not consider so. The tributes he paid me when I was taking leave of him go beyond my dreams.
Smiling at his son Jayanta, who stood by us
And longed for such honors for himself,
Lord Mahendra bestowed on me this garland of Hibiscus,
And anointed me with the sandal paste smeared on his
chest.

MATALI: Such humility is indeed becoming of one who deserves Lord Mahendra's honors.
Today's respite from the harangues of the demons
Relieves the heavens twice of troubles:
Your smooth arrows deployed earlier today,

And long ago, the claws of the Griffin[4].

DUSHYANTA: There lies the greatness of Lord Mahendra.
In employing, for the success of a great task,
An agent, he reveals his esteem for the person.
Could Dawn dispel the darkness of night,
If Sun, of thousand rays, had not engaged him?

MATALI: Your thinking seems to be worthy of your character.
(Having gone a little farther)
Look here, sir. Your glory had spread across to these lands.
The gods of these skies inscribe on the garment,
Made from the Kalpa tree, your good deeds,
With the cosmetic paint of the beautiful nymphs,
And thus celebrate it as the song of an epic drama.

DUSHYANTA: Eager to kill the demons, I had not paid attention to the path of heavens during my ascent yesterday. Matali, would you tell me which way of winds we are descending now?

MATALI: *This region, wherein three streams of the Ganges start,*
Where the orb of lights revolves and shines on all,
Where the god Vishnu strode, sanctifying the path,
Is known as the wind of Parivaha, the dust-free.

DUSHYANTA: So that explains why my exterior and inner being are in soothing harmony.
(Looking at the side of the chariot)
I think we have descended to the region of the clouds.

---

4. Griffin is an incarnation of the god Vishnu.

MATALI: How can you tell?

DUSHYANTA: *The vagrant clouds dart through the spokes like birds,*
The horses gleam in instances of flickering lightning,
The rims of the wheels are sprayed with moisture,
So we must be descending through the rain-pregnant
clouds.

MATALI: And in a few seconds, we shall be over your kingdom.

DUSHYANTA: *(Looking down)*
Since we descend rapidly, how strange the human
world looks, Matali!
Landscape seems to glide off the mountain peaks,
Tree trunks thrust up denuding the cover of leaves,
Rivers, born emaciated, grow stronger and wider.
Do you see it? I feel as if the earth is being offered to me.

MATALI: Sir, you have a keen sight.
(Appreciatively gazing down)
Indeed, how lovely the earth looks!

DUSHYANTA: Matali, what is this mountain range extending
between the eastern and western oceans, drenched
in gold essence like the clouds at sunset?

MATALI: That is Hemakuta, the mountain of the
Kimpurushas. It is the place of ascetics to attain
their final salvation.
The son of the self-born Brahma's progeny Marichi,
Kashyapa, the lord of all creatures,
Whom the gods and demons worship as their master,
Spends his ascetic life here with his wife.

DUSHYANTA: Then let us not ignore the welfare of our spiritual
being. I would like to circumambulate the holy
saint in reverence.

MATALI: A foremost deed, in deed.
                (Acting to descend the chariot)
                There, we are on the land.
DUSHYANTA: *(In surprise)*
                No sound of the contact of the rims of the wheels;
                No heap of the dust stirred from such descent,
                Since there had been no jolt of landing on the earth
                It appears as if the chariot never touched the soil.

MATALI: It is one of unique differences between your chariot
                and Indra's.
DUSHYANTA: Matali, where is the hermitage of Maarichi?
MATALI: *(Pointing with hand)*
                There, where that sage, half-buried in the ant-hill,
                His chest adorned with snakeskin twisted like a thread,
                Around his neck the coiling branches of a dying vine,
                On whose unkempt long locks birds had nested,
                Stands still, like a post, facing the orb of the sun.

DUSHYANTA: I bow to you, Stoic.
MATALI: *(Tightening the reins)*
                There we entered the ashram of Maarichi, fes-
                tooned with the hibiscus trees tended by his own
                wife.
DUSHYANTA: A more heavenly place would not exist! I feel as if I
                plunged into a sea of nectar.
MATALI: *(Stopping the chariot)*
                You can dismount, sir.
DUSHYANTA: *(Dismounting)*
                What about you, Matali?
MATALI: Since I stopped the chariot, I might as well get down.
                (Doing so)
                We will visit a few of the ashrams.

DUSHYANTA: I look at them with wonder.
Here the Kalpa trees breathe out the vital air
That sustains the hermits,
The ablutionary water is golden
With the pollen of lotus;
The saints meditate on diamond slabs, undisturbed,
In the presence of heavenly beauties;
They meditate surrounded by wealth
That every one seeks by doing penance.

MATALI: The prayers of the great in deed aim high.
(Walking around, looking up at the sky)
Venerable Sakalya, how is holy Maarichi at this moment? What did you say? Upon his wife Aditi's request, he is explaining to her the duties of a faithful wife?
(Looking at the king)
Our task must wait a while. Stay in the shadows of the Ashoka tree there. I will go and inform holy Maarichi of your intention to see him.

DUSHYANTA: As you suggest.
(Matali leaves.)

DUSHYANTA: *(Acting out an omen)*
Though my desire is unattainable,
Why does my arm throb in vain?
Earlier I spurned my only salvation
And transmuted it into my misery.

VOICES: *(Offstage)*
No! Don't be naughty. You cannot have it your way all the time!

DUSHYANTA: *(Listening)*
This is not the place for bad behavior. Who could be naughty?

(Looking in the direction of the sound, in surprise)
Oh, it is a child! Two hermit women are trying to restrain him, but he exhibits more strength for his age!
He drags a lion cub, half-suckled at the mother's breast,
Its hair disheveled and tousled in the struggle,
Forcefully against its will,
Wanting to make it his playmate.

(Enter a child as described above followed by hermit women.)

BOY: Open your mouth, lion. I want to count your teeth.
FIRST WOMAN:

Why do you tease the cub? It is a baby as we were once. Because of this, hermits nicknamed you Sarvadamana, the all-conquering.

DUSHYANTA: My heart is drawn towards him as if he is my own. Not having a son makes me tender, I suppose

SECOND WOMAN:

If you do not release the cub, the mother lion would spring on you.

BOY: *(Smiling)*
Mummy, I am frightened!
(He puts forth his tightened lips.)

DUSHYANTA: *The seed of great brilliance I discern in him*
                        Like an ember waiting to erupt into a great fire.

FIRST WOMAN: Dear boy, release the cub. I will give you something else to play with.

BOY: Where is it? Show me.
                        (He holds out his hand.)

DUSHYANTA: He has the birthmark of a universal emperor!
                        Seeking the offered object, he stretches his hand,

Whose fingers are woven like a web,
As if the tight petals of lotus bud was pried
Open by the pink ray of the early dawn.

SECOND WOMAN:

Words alone will not persuade him to stop. Suvrata, go to my hut and get him the clay peacock that belongs to the son of the hermit Markandeya.

FIRST WOMAN:

All right.
(She exits)

BOY: Meanwhile I will play with this.
(He laughs at the hermit woman.)

DUSHYANTA: I feel affection for this naughty child.
When they show their toothless mouth,
In a burst of silly laughter;
When with charm they stutter
In an attempt to speak words;
When they plead to be lifted up
Into the arms of their parent;
Blessed are the fathers who do so
Though dirtied by the dust of their limbs.

SECOND WOMAN:

So, you will not listen to me?
(Looking to the sides)
Are there any hermits here?
(Seeing Dushyanta)
Sir, would you please make this boy release the cub from his tormenting iron grip?

DUSHYANTA: *(Approaching, with a smile)*
Hey, hermit's boy,
Against the rules of this ashram

You act out at such a tender age!
Hermits should commune with all things
Unlike a young cobra that violates its host, the sandal
tree.

SECOND GIRL: He is not a hermit's son, sir.

DUSHYANTA: I should have guessed from his behavior. But then, because of this place, I assumed so.
(Doing as he was asked and touching the boy, to himself)
When I touch this child of another family,
My body is filled with such happiness,
What bliss he would bring to the father
From whose loins he sprang forth!

SECOND WOMAN:
(Looking at both)
That is strange!

DUSHYANTA: What is?

SECOND WOMAN:
You both seem to resemble each other. And though you are a stranger, the boy does not seem to mind at all.

DUSHYANTA: *(Patting the boy)*
If he is not a hermit's son, whose is he?

SECOND WOMAN:
Of Puru.

DUSHYANTA: *(To himself)*
He is of my race! Perhaps, that's why she thought that he resembled me. The people of Puru, in deed, are religiously devout.
When they rule the earth in their prime
They do live in luxurious palaces,
Later in their life, when they observe asceticism,

The roots of trees become their dwellings!

(Aloud)
How could a mortal live in a place such as this?

SECOND WOMAN:

That is true. But this boy's mother, being related to heavenly nymphs, could give birth to him in Maarichi's ashram.

DUSHYANTA: *(To himself)*
My dead hope may be reborn!
(Aloud)
And which royal sage is her husband?

SECOND WOMAN:

Who would like to utter the name of a man who deserted his faithful wife?

DUSHYANTA: *(To himself)*
Such an aspersion is definitely aimed at me. If I asked her the name of the boy's mother, would it be a proper thing to do—asking about another man's wife?
(Enters the first woman with a toy peacock)

FIRST WOMAN:

Sarvadamana, see this lovely Sakunta bird[5].

BOY: *(Looking about)*
Where is my mother?
(Both women laugh)

---

5. She actually uses the conjugate word shakuntalavannam in the colloquial Prakrit language (in Sanskrit it could be deconjugated either as Shakunta [=bird]+laavanyam [=beauty] or Shakuntala+varnum [=color]. A word pun, which is intended to solve the dilemma of the delicate situation. The boy would definitely misunderstand the conjugated word, leading to the disclosure of the mother's name.

FIRST WOMAN:

In his affection towards his mother, he is misled by the similar word.

SECOND WOMAN:

Child, she is only telling you to see the beauty of the clay peacock.

DUSHYANTA: *(To himself)*

What? Is Shakuntala her name? But there could be many instances of Shakuntala as a name. I only wish that this would not be a mirage to break my heart.

BOY: I like this nice peacock.

(He takes the toy.)

FIRST WOMAN:

(Looking, anxiously)

Oh my God, his protective amulet is not on his wrist!

DUSHYANTA: Don't be anxious. Here it is. It must have slipped off his wrist while he was playing with the cub.

(He bends to pick it up.)

BOTH WOMEN:

Do not touch it. Do not touch it. Oh, he has picked it up!

(They stare at each other in astonishment.)

DUSHYANTA: Why did you prohibit me to touch this?

FIRST GIRL: The amulet contains a rare divine herb called Aparajita—the Invincible, and was given by the sage Maarichi to the child at the time of his birth. Only he and his mother and his father might pick it up if it fell on the ground.

DUSHYANTA: If someone else touches it?

FIRST GIRL: It becomes a snake and bites the person.

DUSHYANTA: Have you ever seen it happening?
BOTH GIRLS: Oh, many a time, sir.
DUSHYANTA: *(With joy, to himself)*
    I should be thankful, for my desires might be coming to fruition.
    (He embraces the child.)
SECOND WOMAN:
    Come with me, Suvrata. We must report this incident to Shakuntala.
    (Two women leave.)
BOY: Let me go. I want to go to my mother.
DUSHYANTA: My son, we will both go to your mother.
BOY: Dushyanta is my father, not you.
DUSHYANTA: *(Smiling)*
    That objection strengthens my position.
    (SHAKUNTALA enters; her hair dressed in a single braid.)
SHAKUNTALA: When I heard the account of how Sarvadamana's amulet remained unchanged, when a stranger picked it up, I thought I could not trust my good fortune. But from what Sanumati told me, it might be true.
DUSHYANTA: *(Looking at Shakuntala)*
    There she is!
    She is wearing the saffron-colored bark clothes.
    Her face is thin with the penance, her hair worn in a single braid.
    She is truly pure-minded, though I have been cruel to her,
    She still observes the long separation from me!

SHAKUNTALA: *(Looking at the remorseful king)*

He could not be my husband. Then, who could have defiled my son against his amulet?

BOY: *(Running to his mother)*

Mother, this man calls me his son.

DUSHYANTA: The cruelty I had shown you strikes me now. I see that now it is I that should be recognized.

SHAKUNTALA: *(To herself)*

Breathe slowly my heart. Breathe slowly. Unkind Fate has finally taken pity on me. That is really my husband.

DUSHYANTA: My dear,

Memory has broken the darkness of my delusion
When I see my beloved standing in front of my eyes;
The eclipse being over, Rohini would once again
Join in delight with her consort, the Moon.

SHAKUNTALA: Victory, Victory to...

(She breaks off, choked with tears)

DUSHYANTA: Beloved,

Though tears kill the words of victory,
I have already won the victory
When I saw before me your face
With those pale and unadorned lips.

BOY: Who is he, mother?

SHAKUNTALA: Ask providence, my son

(She weeps.)

DUSHYANTA: *(He falls at the feet of Shakuntala)*

Banish the sad thoughts of my rejection from your heart,
I acted cruelly under the spell of a delusion.
Under its dark influence I did not recognize the good
fortune

Like a blind man, who rips a garland as if it were a snake!

SHAKUNTALA: Rise, my husband! I should have done something bad in my former life, which spent its force now. Otherwise, a compassionate person like you would not have acted that way.
(The king rises.)
How did you come to remember this wretched girl?

DUSHYANTA: I will tell you once this feeling of sorrow passes over.
In my delusional state, I ignored to wipe
The tear drop that afflicted your lip before;
Now, let me cleanse my remorse
By wiping it while it still clings to the lashes.

(He does so.)

SHAKUNTALA: *(Noticing the royal signet ring)*
My dear, this is the ring.

DUSHYANTA: Yes, this is the ring that brought my memory back to me.

SHAKUNTALA: So this ring did what I failed to convince you of then.

DUSHYANTA: Let the vine receive the blossom now to proclaim its union, as it is the season of spring.

SHAKUNTALA: I do not trust the ring. You should wear it.
(Enter Matali)

MATALI: Felicitations to your reunion with your wife and your son!

DUSHYANTA: A friend has brought about the fulfillment of desires. Could Indra have known that this would happen?

MATALI: *(Smiling)*
There is nothing hidden from the gods. Come now. Maarichi has granted an audience.

DUSHYANTA: Shakuntala, take the child's hand. I like you to
                come along to see Maarichi.

SHAKUNTALA: But, I am shy of appearing before my elders with
                my husband!

DUSHYANTA: It is the proper thing to do on a happy occasion like
                this. Let us go.
                (All walk around.)
                (Enter Maarichi, sitting on a throne, and his wife Aditi)
                Aditi,
                There you see him, who leads your son Indra's battles.
                He is called Dushyanta, the lord of the world.
                Because of his bow, the thunderbolt of Indra rests,
                Without a task for it, like an ornament.

ADITI: One could tell from his appearance his inner majesty.

MATALI: The parents of the gods look at you with the
                parental affection. Approach them, sir.

DUSHYANTA: *The cause of twelve-fold energy as declared by the sages,*
                The progenitors of the Lord that rules three worlds and
                the gods,
                In whom Vishnu higher than Brahma effected his birth,
                Born of Marichi and Daksha, close to the Creator, is
                this the couple?

MATALI: Yes, this is that couple.

DUSHYANTA: *(Prostrating before them)*
                The servant of Indra, Dushyanta, salutes you both.

MAARICHI: Long may you rule the earth!

ADITI: May you be without a rival!

SHAKUNTALA: With my son, I bow to you both.

MAARICHI: Dear,
                Your husband is Indra's equal, your son Jayanata's,

Thus, befittingly: may you be like Paulomi!

ADITI: May you be your husband's beloved! May your son
                  live long, bringing esteem to both your families!
                  Be seated.
                  (All sit down near Maarichi.)

MAARICHI: *(Looking at each)*
                  I look at Shakuntala, the faithful wife,
                  The son and you, the virtuous ruler,
                  I feel as if Faith, Wealth, and Duty
                  Have met here in a happy union.

DUSHYANTA: First our wishes come true. Then, you favor us with
                  your audience. This is indeed a unique blessing. As:
                  The flowers blossom before the fruit,
                  The clouds gather before the rain.
                  This is the natural law of the Cause and Effect.
                  But, our good fortune precedes your blessings!

MATALI: That's how universal benevolence flows!

DUSHYANTA: Venerable Sage, I married first your handmaid,
                  Shakuntala, by the ceremony of Gandharva and
                  then refused to acknowledge her when she was pre-
                  sented before me by her relatives, for some odd loss
                  of memory. In doing so, I have committed a blun-
                  der to one of your lineage, that of Kanva. After I
                  saw this signet ring, I remembered that I had mar-
                  ried her. It seems to be very strange:
                  When an elephant went by my very eyes
                  I would not believe, as if it did not happen,
                  But, afterwards looking at the foot prints
                  I was convinced. A strange state of mind!

MAARICHI: Son, do not blame yourself. Your delusion was imposed upon you. I will explain.

DUSHYANTA: I am listening.

MAARICHI: When the nymph Menaka brought her daughter from the pool of Nymphs, to my wife, in a state of total collapse, by meditative powers I gathered what had happened. You disowned her, because of a curse put on her by the sage Durvasa. The curse would have spent its force upon your seeing the ring.

DUSHYANTA: *(With a sigh of relief)*
               Those words free me.

SHAKUNTALA: *(To herself)*
               Then, my husband had no intention of spurning me. He genuinely did not remember me. I must have been so preoccupied with the thoughts of separation that I did not hear the curse at all. My friends had indeed cautioned me to show the ring if something went wrong.

MAARICHI: Daughter, now that you have learnt the facts, you should bear no resentment against your husband. Because:
               Your husband repudiated you
               When the curse clouded his mind;
               That darkness is removed now
               And he is for you to command,
               When a mirror is covered with dust,
               A reflection is not possible,
               But when its surface is clean,
               It reflects a sharper image.

DUSHYANTA: As you say, venerable sage.

MAARICHI: I hope you will welcome your son, born to Shakuntala, and whose birth ceremonies I carried out myself.

DUSHYANTA: In him lies the continuity of my lineage.
(He holds the boy by his hand.)

MAARICHI: Because of his temperament, he would become an emperor.
In his chariot, crossing smoothly the oceans,
He would rule the seven continents unopposed.
Known here as Sarvadamana as he subdues all beasts,
He shall be known as Bharata, the bearer of the world.

DUSHYANTA: Since your holiness performed his birth rites, I have great hopes for him.

ADITI: Now that Shakuntala's wishes are fulfilled, her father Kanva must be informed of this account. Her mother Menaka is also here on my attendance.

SHAKUNTALA: *(To herself)*
Her Holiness has voiced my heart's wish.

MAARICHI: By his meditative powers, Kanva knows of everything that had happened.

DUSHYANTA: Perhaps that is why he did not unleash his anger upon me.

MAARICHI: However, it is appropriate to inform him of this. Is any one there?
(Enter a disciple)

DISCIPLE: I am here, Your Holiness.

MAARICHI: Galava, fly at once to the reverend Kanva. Report to him as my words the merry news that his daughter Shakuntala was blessed with a son. She was also accepted by the King Dushyanta, who recognized her after the curse was lifted off.

DISCIPLE: As you command, Your Holiness.
(He leaves.)

MAARICHI: Son, take your wife and your son, and go to your capital in Indra's chariot.

DUSHYANTA: As you command, Your Holiness.

MAARICHI: Now,

Let Indra bless you and your subjects with prosperity.
You in turn please the gods by your worship!
Let this cycle of blessings and worships be followed,
Reciprocating the good with good for the benefit of god
and man.

DUSHYANTA: I shall try my best for such welfare, Your Holiness.

MAARICHI: Son, what further help may I offer you?

DUSHYANTA: There is no greater favor. If it pleases Your Holiness, let me say this:

(Curtain Call)

Let the monarch work for the welfare of his subjects,
Let the words of the learned and wise be esteemed,
Let Lord Shiva, of blue throat, the self-born, of vast
powers
Liberate me from the cycle of my rebirths.

(All Exit)

CURTAIN

THE END

About the Author

G. N. Reddy was born in Madras, India in 1961. Since 1983, he has been living abroad, mostly in the USA and Europe. He is a scientist by profession, but he strongly believes in the redeeming qualities of both Science and Literature for the humanity. His other works include the novel, When Maples Blush. He lives in New York City with his wife.

He can be reached by email at: gn.reddy@usa.net

Printed in the USA
CPSIA information can be obtained
at www.ICGtesting.com
BVHW042219130823
668494BV00001B/57